√

Shakespearean Staging, 1599-1642

Shakespearean Staging, 1599·1642

T. J. King

Harvard University Press
Cambridge, Massachusetts · 1971

For Joan

Acknowledgments

I hope my extensive indebtedness to earlier scholarship is clearly indicated in the notes. Here it is a pleasure to offer thanks to those who have aided my study in a more personal way. I am grateful to S. F. Johnson and William W. Appleton of Columbia University and Alfred Harbage of Harvard University for their encouragement in the early stages of this investigation, and to Samuel Schoenbaum of Northwestern University, C. Walter Hodges, and Ifan Kyrle Fletcher for their help in the publication in article form of some of my findings. I am also greatly indebted to the expert opinions of those who read the manuscript: Gerald Eades Bentley of Princeton University, Richard Hosley of the University of Arizona, Robert Grams Hunter of Dartmouth College, and Tom T. Tashiro of the City College of New York. For research and clerical help I am grateful to Greg Audette, Karin Bergstrom, Mrs. Rhona Charkey, Mrs. Rachel Gilman, and Mrs. Jo Watkins.

The authorities of the Columbia University Library, Dartmouth College Library, J. Pierpont Morgan Library, New York Public Library, and Carl H. Pforzheimer Library have given unfailing and courteous help. Prompt and considerate attention to my requests for microfilms was extended by the authorities of the British Museum, Folger Shakespeare Library, Henry E. Huntington Library, National Library of Scotland, University Microfilms, and the Printer to the University, Oxford.

Words are insufficient to express my gratitude to my wife and family for their love and patience on the long road this work has traveled since its inception.

T.J.K.

New City, New York
April 1970

Contents

Illustrations

IV. Frontispiece of *The Wits, or Sport upon Sport,* 1662, a collection of drolls probably acted in the Commonwealth or early Restoration periods. Because of its late printing, this is usually considered to have less significance than the other drawings. See George F. Reynolds, *The Staging of Elizabethan Plays at the Red Bull Theatre, 1605–1625* (New York: Modern Language Association, 1940), p. 30.

THE HUNTINGTON LIBRARY, SAN MARINO, CALIFORNIA

V. Plan and elevation of Trinity Hall, Aldersgate Street, London. The drawing is dated 1782, when the hall was in use as a nonconformist chapel, but Charles T. Prouty maintains that it was built before 1446. Accounts of the Churchwardens of St. Botolph without Aldersgate show receipts from the rental of Trinity Hall to "dyverse players" or "for playes" in seven of the years between 1557 and 1567. See Prouty, "An Early Elizabethan Playhouse," *Shakespeare Survey,* 6:64–74(1953). Though the late date of this drawing makes it difficult to accept all its details at face value as evidence of the Elizabethan stage, Trinity Hall may be similar in design to some of the halls at which pre-Restoration companies played.

GUILDHALL LIBRARY, LONDON

VI. The great hall screen of Hampton Court Palace, built 1531–1536, where the King's men acted *Othello* on 8 December 1636 and *Hamlet* on 24 January 1636/7. Chambers, *WS,* II, 353. The hall screens at Hampton Court and the Middle Temple are discussed fully by Richard Hosley, "The Origins of the Shakespearian Playhouse," in *Shakespeare 400,* ed. James G. McManaway (New York: Holt, Rinehart and Winston, 1964), pp. 29–39.

COPYRIGHT RESERVED

VII. The hall screen of the Middle Temple—originally built in 1574, damaged by enemy action during World War II, and later reconstructed exactly—where *Twelfth Night* was acted on 2 February 1601/2. Chambers, *WS,* II, 327–328.

THE HONOURABLE SOCIETY OF THE MIDDLE TEMPLE, LONDON

VIII. Drawings by Inigo Jones for the remodeled Cockpit-in-Court, made no later than 1628 or 1629. The date and authenticity of the drawings are established by records from the Office of the Works during the period 1 October 1629 to 30 September 1630. A bill presented by the King's men for performances at Court indicates that they first used the renovated building on 5 November 1630, when they offered "An Induction for the House, and the Madd Lover." Court records for 1638 reveal that among the plays performed there were "ould Castel" on 29 May, "Ceaser" on 13 November, and "The mery wifes of winsor" on 15 November. Chambers, *WS,* II, 353. See also Bentley, VI, 267–284; D. F. Rowan, "The Cockpit-in-Court," in *The Elizabethan Theatre,* ed. David Galloway (Toronto: Macmillan of Canada, 1969), pp. 89–102; Glynne Wickham, "The Cockpit Reconstructed," *New Theatre Magazine,* 7:26–36 (Spring 1967); W. de Kuyper, "Two Mannerist Theatres," *New Theatre Magazine,* 9:22–29 (Summer 1969).

WORCESTER COLLEGE LIBRARY, OXFORD

IX. Drawings by Inigo Jones and John Webb for an unidentified pre-Restoration playhouse. See D. F. Rowan, "A Neglected Jones/Webb Theatre Project: 'Barber-Surgeons Hall Writ Large,'" *New Theatre Magazine,* 9:6–15 (Summer 1969).

WORCESTER COLLEGE LIBRARY, OXFORD

Shakespearean Staging, 1599-1642

Short Titles and Abbreviations

Adams, *Herbert* — Joseph Quincy Adams. *The Dramatic Records of Sir Henry Herbert, Master of the Revels, 1623–1673*. New Haven: Yale University Press, 1917.

Bald, *Folio* — R. C. Bald. *Bibliographical Studies in the Beaumont & Fletcher Folio of 1647*. Supplement to the Bibliographical Society's Transactions, No. 13, 1938 (for 1937).

Bentley — Gerald Eades Bentley. *The Jacobean and Caroline Stage*. 7 vols. Oxford: Clarendon Press, 1941–1968.

Bowers, *Dekker* — Fredson Bowers, ed. *The Dramatic Works of Thomas Dekker*. 4 vols. Cambridge: Cambridge University Press, 1953–1961.

Bowers, *B & F* — Fredson Bowers, ed. *The Dramatic Works in the Beaumont and Fletcher Canon*. Vol. I. Cambridge: Cambridge University Press, 1966.

Chambers — E. K. Chambers. *The Elizabethan Stage*. 4 vols. Oxford: Clarendon Press, 1923.

Chambers, *WS* — E. K. Chambers, *William Shakespeare: A Study of Facts and Problems*. 2 vols. Oxford: Clarendon Press, 1930.

Greg, *Bibliography* — W. W. Greg. *A Bibliography of the English Printed Drama to the Restoration*. 4 vols. London: The Bibliographical Society, 1939–1959.

Greg, *Documents* — W. W. Greg. *Dramatic Documents from the Elizabethan Playhouses*. 2 vols. Oxford: Clarendon Press, 1931.

Greg, *Folio* — W. W. Greg. *The Shakespeare First Folio*. Oxford: Clarendon Press, 1955.

Harbage — Alfred Harbage. *Annals of the English Drama 975–1700*. 2nd. ed., revised by Samuel Schoenbaum. Philadelphia: University of Pennsylvania Press, 1964.

HLQ	*Huntington Library Quarterly*
JEGP	*Journal of English and Germanic Philology*
MLN	*Modern Language Notes*
MSR	Malone Society Reprints
N & Q	*Notes and Queries*
PBSA	*Papers of the Bibliographical Society of America*
RenD	*Renaissance Drama*
RES	*Review of English Studies*
RORD	*Research Opportunities in Renaissance Drama*
SB	*Studies in Bibliography*
SQ	*Shakespeare Quarterly*
TN	*Theatre Notebook*

1 Introduction

Offered here is a systematic survey of theatrical requirements for 276 plays first performed by professional actors in the period between the autumn of 1599, when Shakespeare's company probably first acted at the Globe,[1] and 2 September 1642, when the theaters were closed by order of Parliament. My purpose is to provide a clearer picture than has heretofore been available of how the plays of Shakespeare were acted by his contemporaries.

Recent studies of Shakespearean stagecraft suggest widely divergent and sometimes mutually contradictory theories about the equipment needed for pre-Restoration performances (see Appendix A). These conflicts arise because consistent criteria for evaluating the evidence are not applied. Despite the paucity of extant pictorial evidence, it is rejected wholly or in part. Scanty use is made of textual evidence, or else primary emphasis is placed on arbitrary selections of such evidence, which in some cases are of questionable validity for the study of staging. My central aim, therefore, is to seek positive correlations between the external evidence, as provided by contemporary architecture and pictures of early English stages, and the internal evidence, as provided by the texts of plays first performed in the years 1599–1642. The method of evaluating textual evidence includes two unique features. First, for each play cited, summaries are given of all available performance records from late 1599 until 2 September 1642. Second, for plays first acted in this period and first printed in the years 1600–1659, account is taken of bibliographical

1

and textual studies which attempt to discriminate between texts that may depend on playhouse copy and those that probably do not.

Although the preservation of early performance records is largely a matter of historical accident, it is clear that in these years Shakespeare's plays were acted not only at the first and second Globe but also at a minimum of six other places in the London area: Blackfriars, the Middle Temple, Whitehall, St. James, Hampton Court, and the Cockpit-in-Court. For Shakespeare's company—first known as the Lord Chamberlain's men, which in 1603 became the King's men—Court performances were prestigious and lucrative engagements, especially in the reign of James I. It therefore seems likely that when Shakespeare wrote his plays, he had in mind not only the Globe but also the several royal entertainment halls. Other companies also acted at these Court halls and at some of the same provincial towns where Shakespeare's company acted on its frequent tours.[2]

During the period 1599–1642 the royal and courtly influence on the drama increased and, as G. E. Bentley observes, a social cleavage developed in the London audiences.[3] The gentry and professional classes went to enclosed private playhouses such as Blackfriars and the Phoenix, while the lower classes went to open-air public playhouses such as the Globe and the Red Bull. Although these two kinds of playhouse differed in outward appearance, analysis of 276 plays probably first acted by professionals in this period shows that there were no significant differences in the staging requirements of the various companies and that the stage equipment needed was much simpler than has been thought. This study is therefore organized according to the increasing complexity of stage facilities required by the plays rather than according to the playhouse or the acting company. The plays fall into four groups, each with similar staging requirements.

The eighty-seven plays with the simplest requirements can be acted in any hall or playhouse with only minimal equipment: floor space in front of an unlocalized façade with at least two entrances through which large properties can be *brought on* or *thrust out*. Thirty of these plays were acted by the King's men; fifty-seven were performed by other companies.

In addition to entrances and large properties, forty-five plays need an acting place above the stage, which usually functions as an observation post for one or two brief scenes. Nineteen of these plays were acted by the King's men; twenty-six were acted by other companies.

One hundred and two plays require an accessory stage space covered by doors or hangings where actors can hide, or where actors, large properties, or both, can be *discovered*. Here *discover* has the sense of "to disclose, or expose to view (anything covered up or previously unseen) to reveal, show." Fifty of these plays were acted by the King's men; fifty-two were acted by other companies. Of the 102 plays, forty-six also need an acting area above the stage.

Finally, forty-two plays require a trap to a place *below*, which necessitates a platform stage. Twenty-two of these plays were acted by the King's men; twenty were acted by other companies. Of the forty-two plays, twenty-two also need an acting area above the stage, while thirty-two require a covered accessory space.

Nicholas Rowe's edition of Shakespeare (1709) and most subsequent editions add designations of locale to the stage directions at the start of every scene, but these sophistications have no authority. Furthermore, Shakespeare's scenes are seldom precisely localized by the dialogue. In this connection it is important to note that the nine façades of pre-Restoration stages reproduced here share the significant characteristic of being placeless. None of them represents a specific locale, as do the drawings of the tragic, comic, and pastoral settings for the Italian stage in Serlio's *Architettura* (1551).[4] Shakespeare and most other English dramatists of this period follow the convention that for some scenes a nonrepresentational stage may gain temporary localization by a dialogue reference or by functional properties, such as a bed or a banquet, but when the stage is cleared of actors and properties, any designation of place that may have been suggested by the preceding scene is automatically nullified.

The nine façades reproduced here are generally accepted as pictorial and architectural evidence concerning the English pre-Restoration stage. These façades are of two basic designs: doorways and an open space above, as shown in the Swan drawing, the hall screens at Hampton Court and the Middle Temple, the plans by Inigo Jones for the Cockpit-in-Court, and the Inigo Jones/John Webb drawings (Plates I, VI, VII, VIII, and IX); a gallery above with curtains hanging from its lower edge, as shown in the *Roxana, Messalina,* and *Wits* drawings (Plates II, III, and IV). The last two drawings also show curtains on the gallery above. The scale drawing of Trinity Hall (Plate V) shows an overhanging gallery at the western end. Charles T. Prouty suggests that curtains were hung from the lower edge of this gallery to enclose a tiring house or backstage "within."[5]

Either of these basic designs can, with minor adjustments, provide a suitable façade in front of which to act all of the texts that may depend on prompt copy from an English professional company in the years 1599–1642. If a play requires hangings and is to be acted in a hall with doorways and a bare façade, hangings can be fitted over one or more of the doorways, perhaps for special scenes only. Evidence for this procedure is found in Philip Massinger's *The City Madam,* a King's men play first acted in 1632 and printed with variant title pages, some dated 1658, others 1659. This text was apparently printed from prompt copy. Notations appear in the margins of the printed text just as they appear in the margins of some playhouse documents: *Whil'st the Act Plays, the Footstep, little Table, and Arras hung up for the Musicians* (IV.iv) and *Musicians come down to make ready for the song at Aras* (V.i).

No door frames are shown in the stage façades of the Trinity Hall, *Roxana, Messalina,* and *Wits* drawings, but a "door" in the sense of "a passage into a building or room; a doorway," can be provided by parting the hangings at the center opening or at either end. One stage direction suggests that a movable door can be represented figuratively and need not be a literal part of the stage setting. James Shirley's *Love's Cruelty* (Q1, 1640)—licensed for the Queen's men in 1631 and protected for Beeston's boys (young successors to the Queen's men) in 1639—carries the direction *Hippolito seemes to open a chamber doore and brings forth Eubella* (IV).

The nucleus of the textual evidence for this study is the eighteen extant playhouse documents, including promptbooks, manuscripts dependent on playhouse copy, and printed plays with manuscript prompter's markings, for plays first performed by professionals in the period between late 1599 and 1642. The significance of such documents is stressed by Sir Walter Greg:

> But though it is desirable to point out the caution needed in arguing from a restricted number of extant documents, it would be a serious error not to recognize their great importance for criticism. Every item of historical evidence performs a two-fold function: positively it enlarges the basis we have to build on, and enables us to extend the structure of valid inference; negatively it is often

of even greater service in limiting the field of admissible conjecture. That is why to a certain type of mind all fresh evidence is so extremely distasteful. In the present case, when we have made reasonable allowance for individual variation, the documents we are considering afford a very considerable and very valuable body of evidence.[6]

The stage directions in these playhouse documents not only provide authentic information concerning actual performance procedures but also serve as touchstones by which to form hypotheses about the extent to which a given text may depend on playhouse copy. Although scholars attempting to determine the substantive text of a play usually regard playhouse emendations as nonauthorial corruptions, these markings are a valuable source of evidence for the stage historian.[7] I therefore give priority to the available prompt or theatrical versions, even though in some cases the nontheatrical texts of these plays may have greater authority. In general, the scholars I cite concerning the probable source of printer's copy for a given play accept the criteria established by R. B. McKerrow for inferring playhouse provenance of a text:

> What are the characteristics of a prompt-copy of a play, that is to say of a copy used or prepared for use at a theatre by a prompter or stage-manager? Fortunately there can be little doubt as to this, for we have a few manuscripts which undoubtedly represent prompt-copies, as well as several printed plays which correspond so closely in certain peculiarities with these that it seems clear that they must have been printed either from actual prompt-copies or from close transcripts of them. It is true that none of these are very early, but there seems no reason for supposing that there would be any essential difference between prompt-copies of, say, 1590 and of 1620 or 1630.
>
> In a genuine prompt-copy we should expect to find some of the following things:
>
> 1. Warnings, either of actors who are to be ready for entry, or of properties which are required for use later. Thus in the manuscript of *Believe as you List*, two actors are to be "ready to open the Trap doore for Mr. Taylor," Antiochus is to be "ready: vnder the stage," others are to be "ready for the song at ye Arras," and so on . . .
>
> 2. A second mark of genuine prompter's copies is the mention, at the time of the entry of a character, of properties which he will require later in the scene, but either must not or need not exhibit to the audience at the time of entry. Thus, in Beaumont

and Fletcher's *Cupid's Revenge*, 1615, at the head of Act v, sc.
iv, we find the direction, "Enter Leucippus with a bloody handkerchief." The purpose of the handkerchief appears some sixty lines
later when Urania is killed and Leucippus displays it stained with
her blood . . .

3. A third mark of prompter's copies is the mention of actors'
names as a *gloss*. This is important. So far as I have noticed, the
name of the actor in a prompt copy always appears *in addition*
to the name of the character, not substituted for it. Thus in *Believe
as you List* we have "Ent: Demetrius—Wm. Pattrick," or "Ent:
Lentulus: Mr. Rob: wth a letter" . . .

4. Finally, a mark of a print from a stage copy is the entry
of characters before the proper time. This I suppose means that
what was intended as a warning to be ready to enter has been
printed as an actual entrance. Thus in *Cupid's Revenge,* which
we have had other grounds for thinking to be printed from a prompt
copy, many of the stage directions are placed much too early.[8]

For some texts, however, scholars cite other characteristics as evidence
that a given text may be wholly or in part dependent on playhouse
copy. In cataloguing the plays for my study, I have taken these conjectures into account, but unless a text shows one or more of the characteristics described by McKerrow, caution requires that it be designated as
possibly rather than *probably* dependent on prompt copy. If the source
of the printer's copy for a given text is a matter of debate, the divergent
scholarly opinions are cited so that the reader may consider two or
more hypotheses in this matter. While conclusions must often remain
tentative, for purposes of discussion each text is assigned to one of two
categories: texts probably or possibly dependent on playhouse copy, and
texts printed with no indication of dependence on playhouse copy.[9]

The significance of playhouse copy for the study of staging is illustrated
by R. C. Bald's discussion of two variant texts of Fletcher's *The Woman's
Prize*. Bald's comments also indicate some of the problems encountered
in attempting to identify the source of copy for a given text. This play
was probably first performed by the King's men in 1611, and it was
protected for them by the Lord Chamberlain's order of 7 August 1641.
A revival in 1633 caused trouble for the company when, "upon com-
plaints of foule and offensive matters" in the play, Sir Henry Herbert,
Master of the Revels, sent a messenger to "suppress" a performance of
the work on 18 October. The players were required to submit the
promptbook for censorship, and after it was "purged of oaths, prophaness

and ribaldrye," it was returned to them on 21 October. Three days later they apologized to Sir Henry, and on 28 November they acted the play before King Charles and Queen Henrietta Maria at St. James, in a performance that was "Very well likt."[10]

Bald collates a manuscript of the play in the Lambarde Collection in the Folger Shakespeare Library with the first printing in the Beaumont and Fletcher Folio of 1647. He points to differences indicating something of the nature of each text:

> The manuscript omits two whole scenes (II.i and IV.i), two other passages of fourteen and seven lines respectively, and eight of three lines or less. On the other hand, the manuscript has eleven passages omitted in the folio, varying in length from half a line to nine lines, and these . . . are, with the exception of two half lines, all such as Herbert might very well have objected to. The manuscript, accordingly, gives the play as cut for acting before Herbert's time; the folio gives a fuller version of the play, but observes the cuts that were made by Herbert in 1633. Whether one is justified in inferring that the Lambarde transcript was made before 1633 is uncertain. On *a priori* grounds, indeed, it seems more likely that it would have been made after the play had been brought to public notice again by the 1633 revival, and that when a private transcript was allowed the scribe was given the older acting version, now supplanted, as his copy, instead of the more recently made prompt-book which had had to submit to Herbert's censorings.[11]

Although it is uncertain when the manuscript was prepared, it is highly probable that the text behind it was acted both before the censorship of 1633 and before Sir Henry became Master of the Revels in 1623. Bald notes minor differences in the stage directions of the two texts that are significant for the study of staging procedures:

> The stage directions in the two texts of *The Womans Prize* show comparatively few variants. The folio omits a couple of exits noted in the manuscript, as well as two directions which describe the action: . . . *and forces the doore open* after the direction at 113.a.ii.4, and *Petruchio rises out of ye coffin* at 122.a.xi.3. Several of the folio directions point more directly to theatrical performance than the corresponding ones in the manuscript: the manuscript omits *with Rosemary* in the opening direction of the play, and *with a pot of Wine* at 97.b.ix.3; and at 103.a.iv.2 has *Enter Livia at one doore, and Moroso at another harkning* where the manuscript has *Enter Liuia, and Moroso (as vnseene by her)*. Two passages suggest, how-

ever, that the text behind the manuscript was one on which performances had been based. At 114.b.v.3 Maria's entrance is indicated
twice, once at the end of a line, and a second time, more boldly in
the left margin. The second, more emphatic, stage direction was
evidently inserted in the original by the prompter and has been reproduced by the scribe. Some interesting alterations occur after
119.b.xi.6. Where the folio reads *Enter Livia discovered abed, and
Moroso by her,* the manuscript reads *Enter Liuia sick carryed in a
chaire by seruants: Moroso by her,* and the necessary alterations
have been made in the text immediately afterwards to make it
accord with the change in production: "draw 'em" at xi.8 becomes
"beare her" and "lie" at 120.b.iii.2 becomes "sitt." The half line
"draw all the Curtains close" at b.ix.4 is omitted in the manuscript,
and the fact that this omission leaves a broken line shows that in the
play, as originally written, production as indicated in the folio was
contemplated, though at some later date the exigencies of the
theatre compelled an alteration.[12]

If Bald's inferences concerning their provenance are correct, these
texts give an example of how an acting company would improvise procedures according to the auditorium and stage properties available to it.
They also indicate that the stage equipment needed for pre-Restoration
plays was not so elaborate or standardized as some theories of Shakespearean stagecraft have suggested.

While texts dependent on playhouse copy provide important primary
evidence for the study of staging, the converse is also true. Texts evidently
not derived from the playhouse have no primary value as evidence for
the study of staging. For example, in the case of a play printed from
the author's foul papers or rough draft, some stage directions may represent the author's intentions not fully realized on stage. Greg describes
the 1623 Folio text of *Timon of Athens* as "printed from foul papers
that had never been reduced to anything like order. . . There is no
record of the play's having been acted, and it is most unlikely that
it ever was. . . Shakespeare's *Timon* is no finished play but an
ébauche."[13] With other plays the author apparently revised for the reader
and sent to the printing house a text that he specified as nontheatrical.
For example, in his prefatory epistle to the 1605 Quarto of *Sejanus,*
Ben Jonson states: "I would informe you, that this Booke, in all numbers,
is not the same with that which was acted on the publike Stage, wherein
a second pen had good share; in place of which I have rather chosen,
to put weaker (and no doubt lesse pleasing) of mine own, then to

defraud so happy a *Genius* of his right, by my lothed usurpation." Here
Jonson clearly distinguishes between two versions of the play: the authorial text he sent to the printer and the now lost theatrical text used
for the play's unpopular and controversial performance.[14] Thus, while
the 1623 *Timon* and the 1605 *Sejanus* are both authoritative texts,
neither should be offered as primary evidence for the study of staging.

Since dramatic texts of the period are of unequal value for purposes
of understanding stagecraft, I cite textual and bibliographical studies
concerning the provenance of each of 117 texts for which such scholarship is available. Evidence suggests that sixty of these texts depend wholly
or in part on prompt copy and that the remaining fifty-seven texts probably do not depend on prompt copy. Evidence is lacking concerning
the provenance of another 159 texts, which I therefore treat as probably
not dependent on prompt copy. The staging requirements of playhouse
manuscripts and printed texts that may depend on prompt copy are
discussed in detail, followed by summaries of the needs of the plays
that probably do not depend on prompt copy.[15]

The source of my checklist for plays first printed in the years 1600–1659
is W. W. Greg, *A Bibliography of the English Printed Drama to the
Restoration*. For the purposes of this study, I eliminated masques,
pageants, and other texts that are not full-length plays in the sense
that Shakespeare's works are plays (see Appendix C). I also eliminated
as evidence any plays probably first performed before late 1599 and
plays for which evidence is lacking or inconclusive concerning a performance by professionals between late 1599 and September 1642 (see
Appendix B).

In the catalog of plays included in each chapter, the following information, if available, is given for each work: title and reference number
appearing in the Order of Plays for Greg's *Bibliography*, author, title
page date of edition cited, and library holding the text examined. External evidence of performance in the years from late 1599 until September 1642 is then noted, including the date of Revels license, mention
in Court records, or other evidence offered by E. K. Chambers or
G. E. Bentley. Two documents from the office of the Lord Chamberlain
are especially useful in assigning certain plays to a specific company:
the order of 10 August 1639 protecting performance rights in forty-five
plays that were part of the repertory of Beeston's boys at the Phoenix;
and the order of 7 August 1641 forbidding the printing of sixty-two

plays without the consent of the King's men, then playing at the Globe and Blackfriars. Although these lists are not specific evidence of performance, they do indicate that the companies considered the plays to have potential value for their active repertories. Lastly the catalog includes: reference works summarizing the historical evidence about each play; information about the acting company and place of performance provided by the title page (TP) of a printed text; for a manuscript, the modern printed transcription cited, if any; and comment by bibliographers or editors as to whether or not the text cited may depend on playhouse copy.

Manuscripts and printed texts are cited by act number or—if the text is so divided—by act, scene, and line number. Otherwise they are cited by signature or page number. Modern printed transcriptions of dramatic manuscripts are cited by page number. Quotations of dialogue and stage directions from manuscripts (or from modern printed transcriptions thereof) are set in roman within quotation marks; stage directions from early printed texts are set in italics. Original spellings are followed, except that turned letters are silently corrected, the "long s" is modernized, and where appropriate, i is substituted for j and j for i, v for u and u for v. Original line divisions are retained only for the staging plot of *Twelfth Night* in Chapter 6. Abbreviations for the names of characters in speech prefixes and stage directions are silently expanded.

2   Entrances and Large Properties

The eighty-seven plays considered in this chapter can be acted in any hall or playhouse with minimal equipment: floor space in front of an unlocalized façade with at least two entrances. There is no need for movable doors or hangings, an acting area above, or a trap to the place below the stage. Stage direction references to *doors* in these plays—and in most plays discussed later—should be glossed in the early sense of "a passage into a building or room, a doorway." For example, a stage direction in *Twelfth Night* reads *Enter Viola and Malvolio, at severall doores* (II.ii), *severall* being used here in the sense of "distinct or apart" rather than "more than two." The only statement about locale in the text of this scene is Viola's comment that she has "since arriv'd but hither" (1.4). As movable doors would serve no function here or elsewhere in the play, it seems likely that *severall doores* should be taken to mean two entrances such as those in the hall screen at the Middle Temple (Plate VII), where the play was acted on 2 February 1601/2.

Open doorways are seen in the hall screen at Hampton Court (Plate VI), as well as in the façade for the Cockpit-in-Court (Plate VIII) and the Jones/Webb drawings (Plate IX). The Swan drawing (Plate I) has two double-hung doors that can be folded back against the façade for plays in which they are not required. If the premise that stage hangings can be parted to provide suitable entrances is accepted, all the plays included in this chapter can be acted on the stages shown in the *Roxana*, *Messalina*, and *Wits* drawings (Plates II, III, and IV). An actor is in fact seen stepping from between the hangings in the *Wits* drawing.

11

*Promptbooks, manuscripts dependent on prompt copy,
and printed texts with manuscript prompter's markings,
for plays first acted by professionals in the years 1599–1642.
Listed in order of presumed date of first performance.*

Measure for Measure (392), Shakespeare, (collection) 1623 (Padua).
King's men at Court, 26 December 1604 (Chambers, *WS,* II, 331).
"We may fairly assume that the copy for F was an edited transcript,
possibly by Crane, but of what is less clear, since the scribe seems
to have edited away most indications of origin. If, however, we suppose, and it is a fair guess, that in the prompt-book something was
done either to remove or to lend substance to the various shadowy
characters, it would seem likely that what the scribe had before him
were foul papers that had been left in rather rough state." Greg,
Folio, p. 356. The Padua copy of the Folio contains contemporary
manuscript prompter's markings. I cite the collotype reproduction in
Shakespearean Prompt-Books of the Seventeenth Century, II, ed.
G. Blakemore Evans (Charlottesville: Bibliographical Society of the
University of Virginia, 1963).

In a more recent study Evans notes: "Evidence is furnished by
a prompt-book of Shirley's *Love's Cruelty* that employs a copy of
the quarto of that play published in 1640. An examination of the
Love's Cruelty prompt-book shows beyond question that the same
prompter-reviser is at work as in the Padua *Macbeth* and *Measure
for Measure.* The handwriting is the same and the principal distin-
guishing characteristics noted for the two Padua prompt-books are
present: no indication of scene settings; non-anticipative calls; indication of the act break; short horizontal line to mark exact point of
entry; prompt calls enclosed between horizontal lines. There is also
a further link offered by actors' initials. On sig. E 1 the role of the
Juggler is assigned to 'T [S]' (cf. *Macbeth,* IV.ii.139, where 'T S'
plays the Doctor), and on sig. F 1v the role of the Servant is assigned
to 'Mr H' (cf. *Macbeth,* IV.ii.64, where 'Mr H[e]wit' plays the part
of a Messenger). Moreover, the same kind of imperative warning
notation ('Bee [ready]/Duke [?Eubella]/Seb: [?Court]') appears on
sig. I 2 as that found twice in the Padua *Measure for Measure* (IV.iii
and V.i.259). . . . I suggest that these four prompt-books belonged
to some kind of splinter group touring in the provinces or abroad

shortly before the closing of the theatres in 1642 or during the inter-regnum." G. Blakemore Evans, "New Evidence on the Provenance of the Padua Prompt-Books of Shakespeare's *Macbeth, Measure for Measure,* and *Winter's Tale," SB,* 20:239–242(1967).

Beggars' Bush (MS), Fletcher, with Massinger? (Folger). King's men at Whitehall, 27 December 1622; King's men at the Cockpit-in-Court, 30 November 1630; King's men at Hampton Court, 19 November 1636; King's men at Richmond, 1 January 1638/9; protected for King's men 7 August 1641 (Bentley, III, 312–318). "The manuscript was clearly transcribed from the theatrical prompt-copy of the play, since it incorporates a number of obvious prompter's directions not to be found in the printed text." Bald, *Folio,* p. 62.

The Parliament of Love (MS), Massinger (Victoria and Albert Museum). Revels license for Phoenix company, 3 November 1624 (Bentley, IV, 805–807). I cite the edition of K. M. Lea, who states: "The [Revels] license has apparently been cut out of the last leaf of the play. . . It would appear that the extant manuscript is actually that submitted to Herbert for license in 1624. . . *The Welsh Ambassador* is written by the same scribe." MSR (London, 1928 [1929]), pp. vi, xi. Greg observes that the stage direction "Ent' Beaupre" is duplicated in the right hand edge of the text: "Ent' Beaupre like a More," which suggests that the MS may have had some use as a prompt-book. Greg, *Folio,* p. 134. But in an earlier work Greg states: "Except for the presumption of the license there is nothing to connect this manuscript with the playhouse." Greg, *Documents,* I, 282–283.

The Soddered Citizen (MS), Clavell (British Museum). Contains King's men cast list ca. 1630 (Bentley, III, 162–165). I cite the edition of J. H. P. Pafford and W. W. Greg, who state: "The only hand recognized [in alterations] is that of a theatrical reviser who added a number of notes and directions. . . The writer has conveniently (though without much reason) been given the name 'Jhon'. . . He was most likely book-keeper of the King's company at least from 1625 to 1631, and the presence of his hand would alone suffice to indicate that company as the owners of the manuscript." MSR (London, 1935 [1936]), p. viii.

Love's Cruelty (573), James Shirley, 1640 (National Library of Scotland). Revels license, 14 November 1631; protected for Beeston's boys, 10 August 1639 (Bentley, V, 1129–1132). TP: Queen Henrietta's men at the Phoenix. See Evans, "New Evidence on the Provenance of the Padua Prompt-Books of Shakespeare's *Macbeth, Measure for Measure,* and *Winter's Tale*," *SB,* 20:239–242(1967).

The Lady Mother (MS), Glapthorne (British Museum). Revels license dated 15 October 1635 at end of text; probably acted by the King's Revels company (Bentley, IV, 483–485). I cite the edition of A. Brown, who states: "It seems likely, in view of the license, the elaborate revisions, the careful preparation of the manuscript for stage use, and the appearance of actors' names on two occasions, that the play was acted." MSR (London, 1958 [1959]), p. xiii.

Plays first acted by professionals in the years 1599–1642 and first printed during 1600–1659 from prompt copy or texts that may depend wholly or in part on prompt copy. Listed in order of first printing.

Patient Grissil (198), Dekker with Chettle and Haughton, 1603 (Huntington). (Chambers, III, 292). TP: Admiral's men. "In spite of various descriptive stage-directions which seem to have held over from the authors' papers, there is some evidence for prompt copy. . . In the nature of the case it might be plausible to conjecture that the actual copy was a transcript of the book rather than the prompt-book itself." Bowers, *Dekker,* I, 210.

King Lear (265), Shakespeare, (collection) 1623 (Columbia). (Chambers, *WS,* I, 463–470). TP (Q1, 1608): "*As it was plaid before the King's Majesty at White-Hall, upon S. Stephens night, in Christmas Hollidaies. By his Majesties Servants, playing usually at the Globe on the Banck-side.*" Kenneth Muir cites some of the widely divergent conjectures concerning the source of printer's copy for Q1 in his Introduction to *The Arden Shakespeare,* 8th ed. (Cambridge: Harvard University Press, 1952), pp. xv–xx. Greg summarizes his own hypotheses as follows: "Q from a careless transcript of foul papers memorially contaminated: F from Q collated with the prompt-book." Greg, *Folio*, p. 427. I have been privileged to examine the unpublished work of Tom T. Tashiro, who offers convincing arguments that Folio *Lear* was set from two copy texts: Apprentice E working from an annotated copy of Q2 (1616), and Compositor B working from a transcript of prompt copy. He further finds that Q1 was set directly from Shakespeare's holograph.

A Fair Quarrel (352), Middleton with William Rowley, 1617 (Huntington). Revels Office records, ca. 1619–20; protected for Beeston's boys, 10 August 1639 (Bentley, IV, 867–870). TP: Prince Charles's (I) men at Court. "Since the 'Additions' [in Issue 2, 1617] are aimed decidedly at spectators rather than readers, they must have been brought to the printer after having been added to the acted play. . . The 'Additions' . . . probably come from a transcrpit of the prompt-book." George R. Price, *"The First Edition of A Faire Quarrell," Library*, 5th ser. 4:141(1949).

A King and No King (360), Beaumont and Fletcher, Q2, 1625 (Huntington). Revels license in 1611; King's men at Court, 26 December 1611 and during 1612–13; King's men at Court, 10 February 1630/1 and 10 January 1636/7 (Chambers, III, 225; Bentley, I, 111). TP (Q1): King's men at the Globe; (Q2): King's men at Blackfriars. "The second quarto, containing many prompt notes, seems to have been printed from the official book which the actors used in the playhouse. . . Similarities [with Q1] seem to suggest that the second quarto was printed from a marked copy of the first. The differences between the two texts suggest, furthermore, that the copy for the second quarto was the official playhouse copy with the prompter's notes." Berta Sturman, "The Second Quarto of *A King and No King*, 1625," *SB*, 4:166(1951–1952).

As You Like It (394), Shakespeare, (collection) 1623 (Columbia). King's men at Wilton, 1603 (Chambers, *WS*, II, 329). "On the whole the evidence points to F having been printed from a prompt-book that retained a few features of the author's papers but had in other respects been carefully prepared." Greg, *Folio*, p. 294.

Twelfth Night or What You Will (396), Shakespeare, (collection) 1623 (Columbia). The Middle Temple, 2 February 1601/2; King's men at Court, 6 April 1618; King's men at Court, 2 February 1622/3 (Chambers, *WS*, II, 327–328, 346). "All things considered it seems most likely that it was the prompt-book (or a transcript of it) that served as copy for F. . . It is almost certain from the insistence on Viola's musical accomplishments at I.ii.57–58 that she was meant to be a singer, and from the awkward opening of II.iv that the song 'Come away, come away death' has been transferred from her to Feste. We must therefore suppose that when the play was originally produced the company had a singing boy who was no longer available on the occasion of some revival. This again would point to the prompt-book having provided the copy for F." Greg, *Folio,* pp. 296–297.

The Spanish Curate (638), Fletcher, with Massinger?, (collection) 1647 (Columbia). Revels license for Blackfriars, 24 October 1622; King's men at Whitehall, 26 December 1622; King's men at the Cockpit-in-Court, 6 December 1638; King's men at Richmond, 7 January 1638/9; protected for King's men, 7 August 1641 (Bentley, III, 417–421; Adams, *Herbert,* p. 49). "[Prompter's directions] are particularly frequent." Bald, *Folio,* pp. 104–105.

The Fair Maid of the Inn (668), Fletcher, (collection) 1647 (Columbia). Revels license for Blackfriars, 22 January 1625/6 (Bentley, III, 336–339). "[There are] several directions in which the hand of the prompter can be discerned." Bald, *Folio,* p. 106.

The Old Law (766), Middleton with Massinger and William Rowley, 1656 (Huntington). Revels Office records, ca. 1619–20 (Bentley, IV, 889–891). TP: Salisbury House and "severall other places." "The quarto of *OL* bears, pretty uniformly throughout, unquestionable marks of having been printed from a promptbook, or a transcript of the promptbook, much more likely the former." George R. Price, "The Authorship and the Manuscript of *The Old Law,*" *HLQ,* 2:125(1953).

The Witch of Edmonton (785), Dekker with Ford and William Rowley, 1658 (Huntington). Prince Charles's (I) men at Court, 29 December

1621 (Bentley, III, 269–272). TP: Prince Charles's men at Court and the Phoenix. "That the manuscript given to the printer had had some connexion with the theatre is shown by the appearance of the names of the actors Theophilus Bird and Ezekiel Fenn after the Prologue and Epilogue respectively, in Bentley's opinion (*Jacobean Stage*, I, 251–252; II, 378; III, 271–272) these representing the speakers and not the writers of the lines. Lines 5–8 of the Prologue suggest to Bentley a revival by Queen Henrietta's men (to which company Bird and Fenn belonged), and he places this event about 1635 or 1636, the manuscript deriving from this occasion." Bowers, *Dekker*, III, 483.

ENTRANCES

Stage directions in the preceding plays indicate that actors enter or exit in different directions, but the entrances are localized only temporarily, if at all. The frequent use of the wording *at one door and . . . at the other* strongly suggests that playwrights of this period thought of the stage as having two entrances. Plays could, of course, be acted in front of a façade with more than two entrances. The Cockpit-in-Court drawing, for instance, shows five doorways (Plate VIII). Only one text that may depend on prompt copy carries directions to suggest the need for a third entrance. *Patient Grissil* has *Enter Urcenze and Onophrio at severall doores, Farnezie in the midst* (G3). The dialogue, however, suggests that Farnezie enters first and observes the meeting of Urcenze and Onophrio. *In the mid'st* may therefore mean that he enters from one of two doorways and stands center stage while he comments on their entrances.[1]

The Soddered Citizen has the following directions: "Enter Brainsick, ffewtricks, Clutch, Shackell, & att t'h'other doare Mountayne hastily &c. Brainsick meetes him wth both hands at his breast &c." (p. 10); "Enter Undermyne at one doare, & att t'hother Mountayne, hastily, in a swett" (p. 48); "Doctor exit at one doare & at thother enter six Creditors servants" (p. 60). In *The Old Law* a direction reads *Enter Eugenia at one Dore, Simonides, Courtiers at the other* (III); *The Fair Maid of the Inn* has *Enter Mariana and Clarissa at one door Cesario at the other* (III) and *Enter Mariana, Clarissa led by two Maides: at the other doore, Baptista meetes with Mentivole led by two Courtiers, the Duke, Bishop; diverse Attendants: (A Song) whilst they salute* (V). *Love's Cruelty* requires that *Hippolito seemes to open a chamber doore and brings forth Eubella* (IV).

Some stage directions use the phrase *one door . . . and another*. Here *another* should be taken in its original sense of "one more, one further, originally a *second* of two things." *A King and No King* has *Enter Arbaces at one dore and Gobrias and Panthea at another* (IV).

As in the stage directions for *Twelfth Night*, *severall* is used in the sense of "distinct or apart." *Measure for Measure* has *Enter Duke, Varrius, Lords; Angelo, Escalus, Lucio, Citizens at severall doores* (V.i). *King Lear* has *Enter Bastard, and Curan, severally* (II.i); *Enter Kent, and Steward severally* (II.ii); *Storme still. Enter Kent, and a Gentleman, severally* (III.i). *Love's Cruelty* has *Enter Bellamente and Bonaldo at severall doores* (IV).

I interpret the direction *over the stage* to mean "enter at one door and exit the other."[2] *King Lear* has *Alarum within. Enter with Drumme and Colours, Lear, Cordelia, and Souldiers, over the Stage, and Exeunt* (V.ii). *Patient Grissil* has *Enter Onophrio and Julia walking over the stage* (C5).

LARGE PROPERTIES

These are required infrequently, and rarely are more than two needed in any given play. Most are commonplace household items simpler than many of the properties listed in Henslowe's *Diary* or in the Revels Accounts.[3] They are often described as *brought on* by servants or *set out*, presumably by stage keepers.

Banquets, Tables, Chairs, and Stools. The Beggars' Bush has the prompter's note "table out" (II) and "Enter, three, or foure Boores A table kans and stools sett out" (III). The prompter's anticipatory directions in *The Spanish Curate* call for the preparation of a banquet for the scene that follows: *Chaire and stooles out*, and *A Table ready covered with Cloath Napkins Salt Trenchers and Bread* (V.i). The next scene begins with the direction *The Table set out and stooles* (V.ii). *The Soddered Citizen* has "A Banquett sett, Then enter Doctor Makewell, & Modestina, in a shrowde" (p. 74); "Wittworth brought in by the Doctors people, in a Chaire" (p. 74); and "Wittworth brought on, in a Chaire, with him enter Doctor Makewell, & Modestina followes

Interior of the Swan Playhouse

I. Interior of the Swan Playhouse

III. Vignette from the Title Page of *Messalina*, 1640

II. Vignette from the Title Page of *Roxana*, 1632

IV. Frontispiece of *The Wits, or Sport upon Sport*, 1662

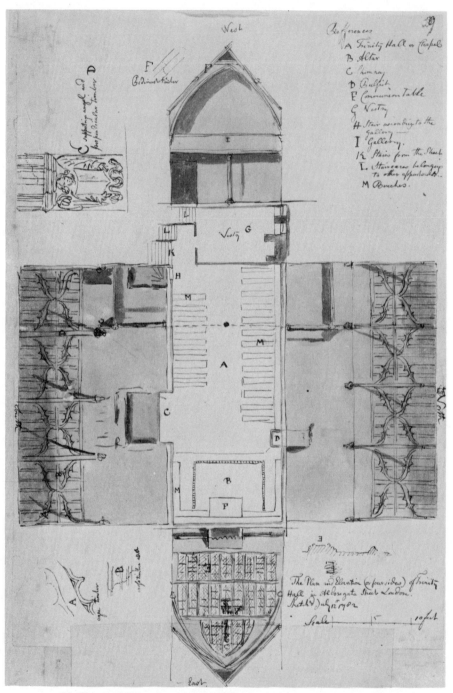

V. Plan and Elevation of Trinity Hall, Aldersgate Street, London

VI. The Great Hall Screen of Hampton Court Palace

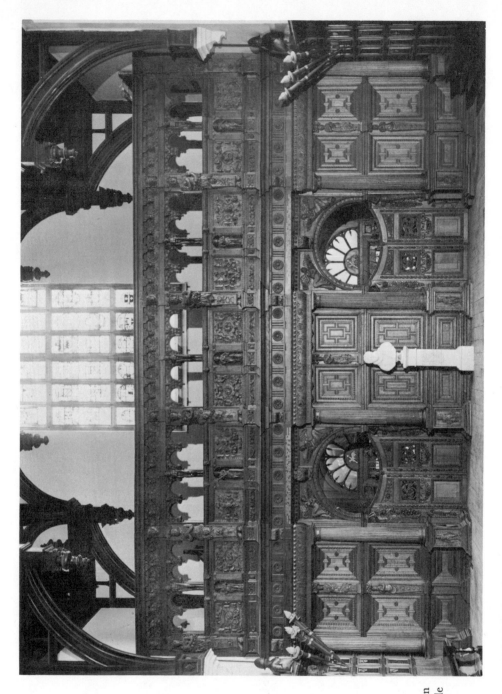

VII. The Hall Screen
of the Middle Temple

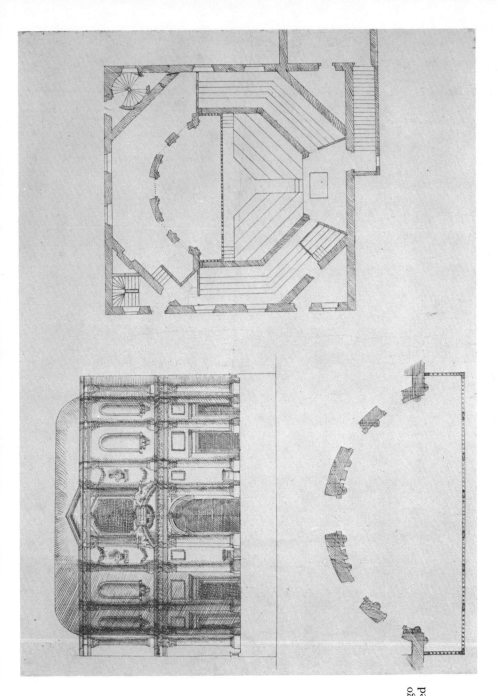

VIII. Drawings by Inigo Jones for the Remodeled Cockpit-in-Court

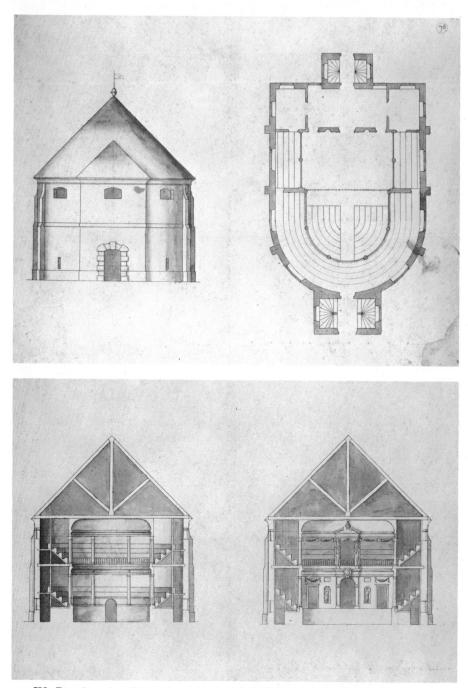

IX. Drawings by Inigo Jones and John Webb for an Unidentified Pre-Restoration Playhouse

after" (p. 89). *King Lear* has *Enter Lear in a chaire carried by Servants* (IV.vii); *The Lady Mother* notes "A Table" preceding the entrance of four actors (p. 92); *Patient Grissil* has *Enter Rees with a company of beggars: a Table is set with meat* (H3v).

Bar. In the final scene of *Parliament of Love,* King Charles of France orders that a trial be held. In the stage directions for the ceremonial entrance is the notation "a barr sett forth" (p. 58). In *The Spanish Curate* a prompter's warning, *The Bar & Book ready on a Table* (III.ii), anticipates the point in the action where these properties are *set out* (III.iii).

Bed. In the margins of *The Spanish Curate* are two prompter's warnings for this property: *Bed ready, wine, table Standish & Paper* (IV.i), and *Diego ready in Bed, wine, cup* (IV.v), which precedes the direction *Enter Diego (in a bed) Millanes, Arsenio, and Parishioners* (IV.v), followed closely by another prompter's note *Bed thrust out.* This indicates that the thrusting out of beds was probably normal procedure even when the stage directions use the term *enter. The Witch of Edmonton* has *Enter Katherine: A Bed thrust forth, on it Frank in a slumber* (IV.ii). *Love's Cruelty* has *Enter Hippolito and Clariana upon a bed* (IV).

Bier, Bodies, Coffin, or Hearse. In the final scene of *The Parliament of Love* the opening stage directions specifies "enter montross on a beere" (p. 58); *King Lear* has *Gonerill and Regans bodies brought out* (V.iii.238); *The Old Law* has *Enter Cleanthes & Hippolita with a hears* (II); *The Witch of Edmonton* has *Father with her in a Coffin* (IV).

Others. King Lear has *Stocks brought out* (II.ii.146).

Other plays first acted by professionals in the years 1599–1642 and first printed during 1600–1659. Listed in order of first printing.

Sir John Oldcastle (166), Drayton, Hathaway, Munday, and Wilson, 1600 (Folger). (Chambers, III, 306–307). TP: Admiral's men.

Cynthia's Revels (The Fountain of Self Love) (181), Jonson, (collection) 1616 (Huntington). (Chambers, III, 363–364). TP: Acted by Chapel Children. Jonson probably revised the text for the 1616 Folio, which follows the neoclassical format indicating a new scene whenever a new character joins the action. This style of notation is not consistent with the practice of theatrical bookkeepers of the period. The 1601 Quarto is also obviously nontheatrical.

The Malcontent (203), Marston with additions by Webster, 3rd ed. 1604 (Huntington). (Chambers, III, 431–432). TP: King's men. "The first edition was set from manuscript, presumably authorial and offering difficulties to the compositor. . . In the third edition the 'Induction' was added, prologue and epilogue were relegated to the end, and many passages were added, while the whole text was reset. The cumulative process of correction throughout this printing history enable an editor to accept some earlier readings . . . [but] a more difficult problem is presented by the omission of stage directions, and the unsure nature of some marginal interpolations." Bernard Harris, ed. *The Malcontent,* (London: Benn, 1967), p. xxxv.

The Fair Maid of Bristow (211), Anonymous, 1605 (Huntington). (Chambers, IV, 12–13). TP: Hampton Court. "Q has very few passages that can accurately represent the lost good text. . . There is a plethora of evidence that Q is a memorial reconstruction." Leo Kirschbaum, *"The Faire Maide of Bristow* (1605), Another Bad Quarto," *MLN,* 40:303,304(1945).

When You See Me You Know Me (212), Samuel Rowley, 1605 (Bodleian). (Chambers, III, 472). TP: Prince Henry's men. "[The] manuscript can hardly have come to [the printer] from the theatre, for entrances and exits are most imperfectly marked, and the quarto bears every sign of having been printed from Rowley's 'foul papers.'" F. P. Wilson, ed., MSR (London, 1952), p. viii.

The Dutch Courtesan (214), Marston, 1605 (Pforzheimer). (Chambers, III, 430–431). TP: Queen's Revels at Blackfriars. "The source of the quarto is almost certainly the author's fair copy or a copy very closely related to it. Although there is no indication of the playhouse in the text, that is, the prompter's hand, the state of the stage directions (centered and marginal) indicates the author's real concern over production." M. L. Wine, ed. (Lincoln: University of Nebraska Press, 1965), p. xxvi.

Sejanus His Fall (216), Jonson, (collection) 1616 (Huntington). (Chambers, III, 366–368). TP (1616): King's men in 1603. Author's epistle in Q (1605) states: "I would informe you, that this Booke, in all numbers, is not the same with that which was acted on the publike Stage." "But although Quarto constitutes an authoritative text, it is superseded by that of the 1616 Folio, which was revised by Jonson in about eighty places as the Volume was going through the press." Jonas A. Barish, ed. *Sejanus* (New Haven: Yale University Press, 1965), p. 205.

All Fools (219), Chapman, 1605 (Pforzheimer). Queen's Revels at Court, 1 January 1605 (Chambers, III, 252). TP: Blackfriars. "All the stage directions . . . are in pompous Latin typical of Chapman's stiff-necked classical yearnings, not the sort of thing one would expect to find in a prompt-book." Frank Manley, ed. (Lincoln: University of Nebraska Press, 1968), p. xix.

Philotas (223), Daniel, 1605 (Huntington). Queen's Revels in 1604 (Chambers, III, 275–276).

The Isle of Gulls (235), Day, 1606 (Huntington). (Chambers, III, 286). TP: Queen's Revels at Blackfriars.

Monsieur D'Olive (236), Chapman, 1606 (Pforzheimer). (Chambers, III, 252–253). TP: Queen's Revels at Blackfriars.

The Phoenix (243), Middleton, 1607 (Pforzheimer). (Chambers, III, 439). TP: Paul's boys at Court.

Cupid's Whirligig (247), Sharpham, 1607 (Pforzheimer). (Chambers, III, 491). TP: King's Revels.

Northward Ho (250), Dekker with Webster, 1607 (Pforzheimer). (Chambers, III, 295–296). TP: Paul's boys. "All in all, though the

evidence is not of the clearest, it would seem that the copy was probably author's papers, perhaps with preliminary prompt markings and
some cuts." Bowers, *Dekker*, II, 408.

A Trick To Catch the Old One (262), Middleton, 1608 (Huntington).
Queen's Revels at Court, 1 January 1608/9 (Chambers, III, 439).
TP: At Paul's, Blackfriars, and at Court.

Your Five Gallants (266), Middleton, 1608 (Pforzheimer). (Chambers,
III, 440). TP: Blackfriars. "There are also two other [characteristics
of foul papers] . . . which are particularly prominent and which would
have rendered stage performance impossible without copious correction
and annotation from the prompter. One is a quite exceptional careless-
ness in the designation of speakers, especially of the minor characters;
the other is the frequent omission of stage-directions, even for the
most obvious entrances and exits." R. C. Bald, "The Foul Papers
of a Revision," *Library*, 4th. ser. 26:39(1946).

The Two Maids of Moreclacke (285), Armin, 1609 (Morgan). (Chambers, III, 210). TP: King's Revels.

The Scornful Lady (334), Beaumont and Fletcher, 1616 (Huntington).
(Chambers, III, 229–230). TP: Queen's Revels at Blackfriars.

Swetnam Arraigned by Women (362), Anonymous, 1620 (Morgan).
(Bentley, V, 1416–1418). TP: Queen Anne's men at the Red Bull.

Thierry and Theodoret (368), Fletcher and Massinger with Beaumont?,
1621 (Pforzheimer). (Chambers, III, 230; Bentley, I, 114). TP:
King's men at Blackfriars. "The characteristics of the print indicate
that [the compositor] was setting from a composite fair copy written
in the hands of the three collaborators which may have been reviewed
and slightly revised by Fletcher. There is nothing to suggest that this
manuscript had served as prompt or that it had been annotated for
transcription into prompt." Robert K. Turner, Jr., "Notes on the
Text of *Thierry and Theodoret* Q1," *SB*, 14:231(1961).

The Deserving Favourite (423), Carlell, 1629 (University of Chicago).
(Bentley, III, 115–117). TP: King's men at Court and Blackfriars.

"All the named roles except servants are assigned to seven adult and three boy actors of the King's company . . . this cast might be taken as evidence that the manuscript came from the playhouse, but the quarto shows none of the characteristics of a prompt copy." Bentley, III, 116.

The Wedding (425), James Shirley, 1629 (Folger). The Quarto gives a list of "The Actors names," all Queen Henrietta's men; protected for Beeston's boys, 10 August 1639 (Bentley, V, 1163–1165). TP: Queen Henrietta's men at the Phoenix.

The School of Compliment (*Love Tricks*) (441), James Shirley, 1631 (Folger). Revels license for the Phoenix, 11 February, 1624/25; protected for Beeston's boys, 10 August 1639 (Bentley, V, 1144–1147). TP: Queen Henrietta's men at the Phoenix.

The New Inn (442), Jonson, 1631 (Pforzheimer). Revels license, 19 January 1628/9 (Bentley, IV, 622–624). TP: "As it was never acted, but most negligently play'd, by some, the Kings Servants . . . 1629."

2 The Fair Maid of the West (446), Heywood, 1631 (Huntington). (Bentley, IV, 569–571). TP: Queen Henrietta's men at Court. "The quarto is generally lacking in stage directions or other features which we recognize as technically theatrical." Robert K. Turner, Jr., ed., *The Fair Maid of the West* (Lincoln: University of Nebraska Press, 1967) p. xix.

Holland's Leaguer (461), Marmion, 1632 (New York Public Library). The Quarto gives a list of actors, all Prince Charles's (II) men; acted six successive days at Salisbury Court, December 1631 (Bentley, IV, 745–748). TP: Prince Charles's (II) men at Salisbury Court.

Changes (462), James Shirley, 1632 (British Museum). Revels license, 10 January 1631/2 (Bentley, V, 1091–1094). TP: King's Revels at Salisbury Court. "If completion of the comedy, Herbert's license, and first production were delayed until January 1631/2, as Herbert's entry suggests, then the King's Revels company for which the play was planned would have left the Salisbury Court before they could use it, but the rights in the play would presumably have remained with the manager of the theatre, who would thereupon have had the play performed by the succeeding company, Prince Charles's (II) men. If the manuscript the printers had was Shirley's, and not a playhouse manuscript, as the state of the text suggests, then the title-page would indicate the intent of the author rather than the fact of production and thus explain the contradiction." Bentley, V, 1093.

The Costly Whore (472), Anonymous, 1633 (Huntington). (Bentley, V, 1312–1314). TP: Revels company.

A New Way To Pay Old Debts (474), Massinger, 1633 (Huntington). Protected for Beeston's boys, 10 August 1639 (Bentley, IV, 800–803). TP: Queen Henrietta's men at the Phoenix.

The Witty Fair One (477), James Shirley, 1633 (Bodleian). Revels license, 3 October 1628; protected for Beeston's boys, 10 August 1639 (Bentley, V, 1166–1167). TP: Queen Henrietta's men at the Phoenix.

A Fine Companion (481), Marmion, 1633 (Pforzheimer). (Bentley, IV, 742–745). TP: Prince Charles's (II) men at Whitehall and Salisbury Court.

A Maidenhead Well Lost (493), Heywood, 1634 (British Museum). (Bentley, IV, 582–583). TP: Queen Henrietta's men at the Phoenix.

The Shepherds' Holiday (499), Joseph Rutter, 1635 (Huntington). (Bentley, V, 1032–1034). TP: Queen Henrietta's men at Whitehall.

A Challenge for Beauty (509), Heywood, 1636 (Pforzheimer). (Bentley, IV, 562–563). TP: King's men at Blackfriars.

The Elder Brother (515), Fletcher, with Massinger?, 1637 (Folger). Blackfriars, February 1634/5; Blackfriars, 25 April 1635; Hampton Court, 5 January 1636/7 (Bentley, III, 332–336). TP: King's men at Blackfriars.

Hyde Park (517), James Shirley, 1637 (Folger). Revels license, 20 April 1632; protected for Beeston's boys, 10 August 1639 (Bentley, V, 1121–1123). TP: Queen Henrietta's men at the Phoenix.

The Young Admiral (519), James Shirley, 1637 (University of Michigan). Revels license, 3 July 1635; Queen Henrietta's men at St. James, 19 November 1633; protected for Beeston's boys, 10 August 1639 (Bentley, V, 1168–1170). TP: Queen Henrietta's men at the Phoenix.

The Gamester (523), James Shirley, 1637 (Folger). Revels license, 11 November 1633; at Whitehall, 6 February 1633/4 (Bentley, V, 1110–1112). TP: Queen Henrietta's men at the Phoenix.

1 The Cid (525), Pierre Corneille, trans. Rutter, 1637 (Huntington). Court performance mentioned in printing license, 12 January 1637/8 (Bentley, V, 1030–1031). TP: Beeston's boys at the Phoenix and Court.

The Fancies (532), Ford, 1638 (Huntington). (Bentley, III, 442–444). TP: Queen Henrietta's men at the Phoenix.

The Royal Master (538), James Shirley, 1638 (Pforzheimer). Revels license, 23 April 1638 (Bentley, V, 1139–1142). TP: New Theater in Dublin and the Lord Deputy's Castle.

Tottenham Court (540), Nabbes, 1638 (Columbia). (Bentley, IV, 940–942). TP: Salisbury Court in 1633.

The Muses' Looking-Glass (547), Randolph, 1638 (Pforzheimer). Revels license for King's Revels company, 25 November 1630 (Bentley, V, 986–989).

Amyntas (548), Randolph, 1638 (Huntington). Revels license for King's Revels company, 26 November 1630 (Bentley, V, 969–971). TP: Whitehall.

Chabot Admiral of France (550), James Shirley with Chapman, 1639 (Columbia). Revels license, 29 April 1635; protected for Beeston's boys, 10 August 1639 (Bentley, V, 1088–1091). TP: Queen Henrietta's men at the Phoenix.

Argalus and Parthenia (557), Glapthorne, 1639 (Huntington). (Bentley, IV, 479–481). TP: Beeston's boys at Court and the Phoenix.

Wit without Money (563), Fletcher, revised by another?, 1639 (British Museum). Queen Henrietta's men at the Phoenix, 10 June 1635; Beeston's boys at Court, 14 February 1636/7; protected for Beeston's boys, 10 August 1639 (Chambers, III, 229; Bentley, I, 250). TP: Queen Henrietta's men at the Phoenix.

Albertus Wallenstein (564), Glapthorne, 1639 (Columbia). (Bentley, IV, 477–479). TP: King's men at the Globe.

Rollo Duke of Normandy (*The Bloody Brother*) (565), Fletcher, with Jonson? revised by Massinger?, 1639 (Folger). King's men at Court, 7 November 1630; King's men at Court, 21 February 1630/1; King's men at the Globe, 23 May 1633; King's men at Hampton Court, 17 January 1636/7 (Bentley, III, 401–407). TP(Q2): King's men.

The Coronation (572), James Shirley, 1640 (Folger). Revels license, 6 February 1634/5; protected for Beeston's boys, 10 August 1639 (Bentley, V, 1098–1099). TP: Queen Henrietta's men at the Phoenix.

The Night Walker (574), Fletcher revised by James Shirley, 1640 (British Museum). Revels license for Queen Henrietta's men, 11 May 1633; at Court, 30 January 1633/4; protected for Beeston's boys, 10 August 1639 (Bentley, III, 384–386). TP: Queen Henrietta's men at the Phoenix.

The Bride (576), Nabbes, 1640 (New York Public Library). (Bentley, IV, 929–932). TP: Beeston's boys at the Phoenix. In preparing the text for printing, the author apparently revised it so as to differ from the version acted; his preface states that *The Bride* "is here drest according to mine own desire and intention; without ought taken from her that my selfe thought ornament; nor supplyed with any thing which I valued but as rags." (A3–A3v)

The Humorous Courtier (577), James Shirley, 1631 (Folger). Revels license, 17 May 1631 (Bentley, V, 1120–1121). TP: The Phoenix.

The Sparagus Garden (587), Richard Brome, 1640 (Huntington). (Bentley, III, 87–89). TP: Revels company at Salisbury Court.

The Ladies' Privilege (590), Glapthorne, 1640 (Huntington). (Bentley, IV, 485–487). TP: Beeston's boys at the Phoenix and Whitehall.

Wit in a Constable (591), Glapthorne, 1640 (New York Public Library). (Bentley, IV, 494–497). TP: Beeston's boys at the Phoenix. "The text . . . shows such marked disturbances as to raise a question as to what the play is." Bentley, IV, 495.

The Hollander (594), Glapthorne, 1640 (Huntington). Revels license for Queen Henrietta's men, 12 March 1635/6. (Bentley, IV, 482–483). TP: Beeston's boys at the Phoenix and Court.

The Magnetic Lady (616), Jonson, (collection) 1641 (Pforzheimer). Revels license, 12 October 1632; Revels Office records, 24 October 1633 (Bentley, IV, 618–620).

The Sophy (622), Denham, 1642 (Pforzheimer). (Bentley, III, 276–279). TP: King's men at Blackfriars.

The Laws of Candy (648), Fletcher, (collection) 1647 (Columbia). (Bentley, III, 354–356). "It has not been possible to find any directions which suggest, even remotely, the specific influence of the prompter." Bald, *Folio*, pp. 109–110.

The Country Captain (681), Cavendish, 1649 (Huntington). Protected for King's men, 7 August 1641 (Bentley, III, 145–148). TP: King's men at Blackfriars.

The Wild-Goose Chase (706), Fletcher, 1652 (British Museum). At Court, Christmas season 1621–21/2; King's men at Court, 24 January 1621/2; King's men at Court, 6 November 1632; protected for King's men, 7 August 1641 (Bentley, III, 425–430). TP: Blackfriars.

The Brothers (723), James Shirley, (collection) 1653 (Columbia). Revels license, 4 November 1626; protected for King's men, 7 August 1641 (Bentley, V, 1082–1084). TP: Blackfriars.

The Sisters (724), James Shirley, (collection) 1653 (Columbia). Revels license, 26 April 1642 (Bentley, V, 1147–1149). TP: Blackfriars.

The Doubtful Heir (725), James Shirley, (collection) 1653 (Columbia). Revels license, 1 June 1640; protected for King's men, 7 August 1641 (Bentley, V, 1105–1107). TP: Blackfriars.

Appius and Virginia (733), Webster, 1654 (Huntington). Protected for Beeston's boys, 10 August 1639 (Bentley, V, 1245–1248).

1 & 2 The Passionate Lover (750 & 751), Carlell, 1655 (Huntington). Part One, King's men at Somerset House, 10 July 1638, King's men at the Cockpit-in-Court, 18 December 1638; Part Two, King's men at the Cockpit-in-Court, 20 December 1638, King's men at the Cockpit-in-Court, 27 December 1638; protected for King's men, 7 August 1641 (Bentley, III, 122–123). TP: King's men at Somerset House and Blackfriars.

A Very Woman (760), Massinger, (collection) 1655 (Pforzheimer). Revels license for King's men, 6 June 1634 (Bentley, IV, 824–828). TP: King's men at Blackfriars.

The Old Couple (784), May, 1658 (Huntington). Revels license, 1636 (Bentley, IV, 839–840).

The English Moor (806), Richard Brome, (collection) 1659 (New York Public Library). (Bentley, III, 67–69). TP: Queen Henrietta's men.

ENTRANCES

At one door and . . . at the other or a similar wording is found in fifteen plays: *The Malcontent* (II.ii, V.iv); *The Fair Maid of Bristow* (C4v); *The Dutch Courtesan* (III.i, IV.i); *Monsieur D'Olive* (I.i); *Cupid's Whirligig* (III, V); *Northward Ho* (II); *A Trick To Catch the Old One* (I); *Changes* (I, II); *The Costly Whore* (IV); *The Witty Fair One* (IV, V); *A Maidenhead Well Lost* (IV); *The Young Admiral* (V); *The Humorous Courtier* (V); *The Sophy* (III, V); *Appius and Virginia* (II, III, V).

Several doors or *severally* appears in seventeen plays: *The Malcontent* (IV.iv, V.i); *The Isle of Gulls* (A2); *A Trick To Catch the Old One* (I); *The Scornful Lady* (I); *Swetnam Arraigned by Women* (II, IV);

The Deserving Favourite (I); *The Costly Whore* (III); *A New Way To Pay Old Debts* (II.ii); *The Witty Fair One* (IV); *The Young Admiral* (III); *Wit without Money* (V); *The Coronation* (II); *The Night Walker* (V); *The Sophy* (IV, V); *The Doubtful Heir* (III); *Appius and Virginia* (II); *1 The Passionate Lover* (V).

Pass over the stage or a similar wording appears in eleven plays: *Sejanus His Fall* (I); *Your Five Gallants* (Prologue); *The Two Maids of Moreclacke* (Hv); *Swetnam Arraigned by Women* (IV.ii); *Thierry and Theodoret* (IV); *Changes* (V); *The Costly Whore* (III, IV); *Amyntas* (V.v); *The Magnetic Lady* (III.ii); *The Doubtful Heir* (IV); *1 The Passionate Lover* (III).

LARGE PROPERTIES

Banquets, Tables, Chairs, and Stools. These are *brought on* or *set out* in fourteen plays: *The Dutch Courtesan* (III.i); *All Fools* (V); *Swetnam Arraigned by Women* (V.ii); *Thierry and Theodoret* (II); *The Deserving Favourite* (II); *The Wedding* (IV); *Rollo Duke of Normandy (The Bloody Brother)* (V.ii); *The Sparagus Garden* (III.iv, IV.iv); *The Magnetic Lady* (III.iv); *The Laws of Candy* (III); *The Country Captain* (IV); *The Doubtful Heir* (IV, V); *The Old Couple* (III, V); *The English Moor* (V.ii).

Bar. One is required in three plays: *Swetnam Arraigned by Women* (III); *Chabot Admiral of France* (II, V); *The Doubtful Heir* (II).

Bed. One is *drawn out* in *A Maidenhead Well Lost* (V) and *drawn forth* in *A Very Woman* (IV). A bed is needed in four other plays, but the texts do not specify how it is introduced: *A Trick To Catch the Old One* (IV); *Thierry and Theodoret* (V); *The Country Captain* (III, IV); *The Wild-Goose Chase* (IV.iii).

Bier, Body, Coffin, or Hearse. One is needed in five plays: *Philotas* (D3); *Monsieur D'Olive* (III); *The Wedding* (IV); *The Costly Whore* (V); *The Witty Fair One* (IV).

Others. An *Altar* is required in *Sejanus His Fall* (V), *Amyntas* (V.v); an *Arbor* in *The Deserving Favourite* (II), *The Witty Fair One* (I);

a *Canopy* in *The Humourous Courtier* (V) ; a *Monument* in *Argalus and Parthenia* (III); a *Seat* in *The New Inn* (III.ii); a *Sedan* in *The Sparagus Garden* (V.vi), *Wit in a Constable* (V); a *State* in *Thierry and Theodoret* (III), *The Coronation* (II); *Stocks* in *The Dutch Courtesan* (IV.i); a *Throne* in *The Doubtful Heir* (V); a *Tree* in *Amyntas* (III.iv); a *Trunk* in *The Two Maids of Moreclacke* (F4), *Tottenham Court* (V.i).

3   Above the Stage

In addition to entrances and large properties, the forty-five plays considered in this chapter need an acting place above the main playing area. Occasionally this space may be described fictionally as a *window* or the *walls*, but more often it is referred to theatrically as *above* or *aloft*. It usually serves during a brief scene as an observation post from which one or two actors comment on, or converse with, actors down on the main stage. This area should therefore be considered as an auxiliary to the main stage rather than a distinct and separate "upper stage." All nine façades in the pictorial and architectural evidence have an elevated area suitable for this kind of limited action.[1]

Promptbook for a play acted by professionals in 1633.

The Launching of the Mary (MS), Mountfort (British Museum). Revels license, 27 June 1633 (Bentley, IV, 922–924). I cite the edition of J. H. Walter, who states: "The license of the Master of the Revels and the annotations by the book-keeper must presumably be taken as evidence of performance. It seems, however, difficult to the point of impossibility to believe that any company would willingly have produced so remarkably unsuitable a play, and we can hardly resist the suspicion that the most it achieved was one or two subsidized

31

performances instigated by, or offered to, the East India Company
and their friends." MSR (London, 1933), p. xi.

Plays first acted by professionals in the years 1599–1642 and
first printed during 1600–1659 from prompt copy or texts
that may depend wholly or in part on prompt copy.
Listed in order of first printing.

Cupid's Revenge (328), Beaumont and Fletcher, 1615 (Huntington).
Queen's Revels company at Court, 5 January 1612/3, 1 January
1613/4, and either 9 January or 27 February 1613/4; Lady Elizabeth's
men at Court, 28 December 1624; Beeston's boys at Hampton Court,
7 February 1636/7; protected for Beeston's boys, 10 August 1639
(Chambers, III, 225–226; Adams, *Herbert,* pp. 52, 57). "A . . . mark
of genuine prompter's copies is the mention, at the time of the entry
of a character, of properties which he will require later in the scene,
but either must not or need not exhibit to the audience at the time
of entry. Thus, in Beaumont and Fletcher's *Cupid's Revenge*, 1615,
at the head of Act V, sc. iv, we find the direction, 'Enter Leucippus
with a bloody handkerchief.' The purpose of the handkerchief appears
some sixty lines later when Urania is killed and Leucippus displays
it stained with her blood." R. B. McKerrow, "The Elizabethan Printer
and Dramatic Manuscripts," *Library,* 4th ser. 12:271(1931).

Othello (379), Shakespeare, (collection) 1623 (Columbia). At the Globe,
30 April 1610; at Court, payment 20 May 1613; King's men at
Blackfriars?, 22 November 1629; at Blackfriars, 6 May 1635; at
Hampton Court, 8 December 1636 (Chambers, *WS,* II, 336, 343,
348, 352, 353). TP (1622): King's men at the Globe and Blackfriars.
"The text of *Othello* was printed in the Folio about August or September 1623, but the copy had doubtless been prepared some while before.
The editors decided to use Q [probably printed from a transcript
of foul papers] to print from, but they seem to have mistrusted the
text—which would be natural if it had been printed from a private
transcript not made under their own supervision—for they insisted
on its being first collated with the prompt-book . . . The collation
generally resulted, therefore, in a considerable improvement of the

text, but at the same time in some not very fortunate reduction of the stage-directions." Greg, *Folio,* p. 371. In her notes, "The Copy for *Othello,* 1622 and 1623," Alice Walker observes: "If we make some allowances for omissions on the part of the F. compositor, either through negligence or for typographical convenience, F.'s stage directions, like its speech prefixes, suggest something more like a fair copy or prompt-book than foul papers." *Othello,* ed. Alice Walker and John Dover Wilson (Cambridge: Cambridge University Press, 1957), p. 129. M. R. Ridley in *The Arden Shakespeare,* 7th ed., (Cambridge: Harvard University Press, 1958), pp. xlii–xliii, expresses skepticism about the possibility that Folio *Othello* depends on prompt copy.

Julius Caesar (403), Shakespeare, (collection) 1623 (Columbia). "Keysar Julio Caesare" at the Globe?, September 1599; King's men at Whitehall, payment 20 May 1613; King's men at St. James, 31 January 1636/7; King's men at the Cockpit-in-Court, 13 November 1638 (Chambers, *WS,* II, 322, 343, 353). "There is one difficulty in supposing that F was printed from a normal prompt-book, namely that we should hardly expect the book-keeper in preparing it to have transcribed the sometimes redundant directions of the author, or to have repeated in the margin directions he had already written elsewhere. Possibly the author for some reason submitted a fair copy of the play—which would also help to account for the cleanness of the text—and that this was used, with some further annotation, as the prompt-book. This would further account for the apparent absence of foul papers in 1623 and the necessity of making a transcript for the printer." Greg, *Folio,* pp. 291–292.

The Antipodes (586), Richard Brome, 1640 (Pforzheimer). (Bentley, III, 55–57). TP: Queen Henrietta's men at Salisbury Court. Author's postscript states: "You shal find in this Booke more then was presented upon the Stage, and left out of Presentation, for superfluous length (as some of the Players pretended) I thoght good al should be inserted according to the allowed Original; and as it was, at first, intended for the Cock-pit Stage, in the right of my most deserving Friend Mr. William Beeston, unto who it properly appertained; and so I leave it to thy perusal, as it was generally applauded, and well acted at Salisbury Court." "The copy for the quarto was almost certainly

the author's papers, or a transcript of these, which had been used
as a theatrical prompt-book." Ann Haaker, ed. (Lincoln: University
of Nebraska Press, 1966), p. xx.

The Custom of the Country (640), Fletcher, (collection) 1647 (Colum-
bia). King's men at Blackfriars, 22 November 1628; King's men at
Hampton Court, 24 October 1630; King's men at the Cockpit-in-
Court, 27 November 1638; protected for King's men, 7 August 1641
(Bentley, III, 324–328). "Anticipatory stage directions." Bald, *Folio*,
p. 105.

The Coxcomb (644), Beaumont and Fletcher, (collection) 1647 (Columbia). Queen's Revels company at Court, 2 or 3 November 1612;
King's men at Court, 5 March 1621/2 and at Hampton Court 17
November 1636; protected for King's men, 7 August 1641 (Chambers,
III, 223–224; Bentley, I, 110). "The copy furnished the printer was
the prompt-book or, more likely, a transcript of it. Although the stage-
directions are not so telling as in other plays of the Folio where they
anticipate entrances and properties, there are several indications of
the nature of the copy." Irby B. Cauthen, Jr., ed., in Bowers, *B &
F*, I, 264.

The Chances (646), Fletcher, (collection) 1647 (Columbia). King's
men at the Cockpit-in-Court, 30 December 1630 and 22 November
1638; protected for King's men, 7 August 1641 (Bentley, III,
318–323). "Actors' names inserted in stage directions . . . anticipatory
stage directions." Bald, *Folio*, pp. 103, 105.

The Loyal Subject (647), Fletcher, (collection) 1647 (Columbia).
Revels license for King's men, 16 November 1618; Revels license
renewal for King's men, 23 November 1633; at Whitehall, 10 December 1633; King's men at Hampton Court, 6 December 1636;
protected for King's men, 7 August 1641 (Bentley, III, 370–373).
"Anticipatory stage directions." Bald, *Folio*, p. 105.

The Queen of Corinth (663), Fletcher, with Field and Massinger?,
(collection) 1647 (Columbia). Protected for King's men, 7 August
1641 (Bentley, III, 398–400). "Evidence is by no means . . . exten-

sive, but it is sufficient to justify . . . conjectural inclusion among the prompt-copies." Bald, *Folio,* p. 108.

Love's Pilgrimage (669), Fletcher, (collection) 1647 (Columbia). Revels license for King's men, 16 September 1635; King's men at Hampton Court, 16 December 1636; protected for King's men, 7 August 1641 (Bentley, III, 366–370). "Actors' names inserted in the stage directions." Bald, *Folio,* p. 103.

The Changeling (712), Middleton with William Rowley, 1653 (Huntington). Revels license for Lady Elizabeth's men at the Phoenix, 7 May 1622; Lady Elizabeth's men at Whitehall, 4 January 1623/4; acted in March 1634/5; protected for Beeston's boys, 10 August 1639 (Bentley, IV, 861–864). TP: Phoenix and Salisbury Court. "The source of the printed text was probably a transcript from theatrical copy." N. W. Bawcutt, ed., *The Revels Plays* (Cambridge: Harvard University Press, 1958), p. xvi. But see also George R. Williams, ed. (Lincoln: University of Nebraska Press, 1966), who finds no convincing evidence for this text having been set from theatrical copy (p. xi).

ABOVE THE STAGE

The Launching of the Mary requires one use by actors of a space above the stage: "after the settinge of the Crabbs, & bendinge of the Cables, there must appeare aloft, as many gallants & ladies as the roome Canne well hold amongst which must be Lo: Ad: Go: Dep: 1.2 Com then enter alowe in haste at one doore, Trunell & tallow, & at another. Tarre, Okum, & Sheathinge nayle" (p. 112). Those above watch the "heavinge at the Capsten," and the scene ends with a general "exeunt"; also, "Musique aloft" (p. 16).

In *Love's Pilgrimage* the action on stage is interrupted by *Enter Roderigo above* (IV.i); he orders a gunner to "make a shot into the Town" and tells the soldiers on stage below to "bring away Antonio into my Cabben." *The Loyal Subject* has *Enter Duke above* (IV.vi); he talks with a group of soldiers assembled below and exits. *The Queen of Corinth* has *Enter Theanor, Agenor, Leonidas above* (IV.ii), and *The Changeling* has *Enter Lollio above* (III) and *Mad-men above, some as birds, others as beasts* (III). *The Antipodes* has *Lefoy, Diana, Joyless appear above* (IV.iv).

In scenes in which actors move backstage from the area above to the main playing area—or vice versa—lines are spoken by those on stage to cover the time elapsing. In *Othello,* Roderigo and Iago call to Brabantio, who appears *Above* at I.i.81 and exits at l. 144. Iago then speaks to Roderigo for sixteen lines and exits, at which point *Enter Brabantio, with Servants and Torches.* In *Julius Caesar,* Cassius orders Pindarus to "get higher on that hill" (V.iii.20) so that he may better see what happens to Titinius; *Pindarus Above* reports that Titinius is "enclosed round about" (1.28).

During a scene in *The Custom of the Country* between Arnoldo and Zenocia, *Enter above Hippolita and Zabulon* (IV); who observe and overhear the conversation of the pair below. Zabulon exits and twenty-nine lines later joins the action on the main stage. A prompter's warning *Bawd ready above* in *The Chances* (IV.ii) anticipates her entrance in the next scene, *Enter Bawd (above).* The actors below observe her but she does not speak; later in the scene she joins the action on the main stage. In the next act appears *Enter Duke, Petruchio below, and Vechio above* (V.i). Vechio overhears the conversation of the characters below but does not reveal his presence to them. Fifteen lines after his last aside to the audience he *enters* and admits the callers. In *The Coxcomb,* Mercury enters, speaks a brief soliloquy, and calls to "this house of sleep," whereupon *Enter a Servingman, above, unready* (II.i). They have a three-line exchange followed by a three-line soliloquy by Mercury before *Enter Servingman.*

In some plays actors apparently remain in full view of the audience as they ascend to, or descend from, the acting area above the stage. For example, *Cupid's Revenge* has *Cornets. Descendit Cupid* (I), followed by a soliloquy of twenty lines and *exit;* later is found *Cornets discend Cupid* followed by an eleven line soliloquy and *exit* (II); toward the end of the play is found *Cornets. Cupid from above* (V), but he speaks no lines until his speech that ends the play several pages later. Of the other texts that may depend on prompt copy, only Shakespeare's *Cymbeline*—discussed in Chapter Five—calls for an elaborate descent: *Jupiter descends in Thunder and Lightning, sitting uppon an Eagle; hee throwes a Thunder-bolt. The Ghostes fall on their knees* (V.iv.92). After his speech of twenty-one lines Jupiter *Ascends.* Although there

is some evidence for elaborate apparatus to "fly" actors and large properties in the Italian theater of the period, evidence for its use in the
English theater is meager.[2] It therefore seems that a more likely means
of staging ascents and descents would be a movable staircase set in
place for the scenes in which it is required. *The Knight of Malta*—a
King's men play ca. 1616—contains a notation apparently printed from
prompt copy: *The Scaffold set out and the staires* (II.v). These are
also mentioned in Henslowe's inventory of properties for the Lord Admiral's men dated 10 March 1598, at which time the company was
playing at the Rose: "i payer of stayers for Fayeton." Henslowe's *Diary*
shows that Dekker was given four pounds for "a booke . . . called
fayeton" on 15 January 1597/8.[3] This text is lost, but if the dramatization
followed the familiar myth, stairs may have been put in place for
Phaeton's ascent to the area above and his subsequent descent.[4]

ENTRANCES

At one door and . . . at the other or similar wording is found in
four plays: *The Launching of the Mary*, "Enter Mary Sparke at one
doore & Isabell Nutt at another with handbaskette" (p. 78); "Enter
dorotea Constance at one doore, at another doore, a servingman who
[gives] her a letter" (p. 86); "Enter at one doore. Lord Admiral: at
another door Governor: Deputy: 1. 2. Comittee" (p. 96); in *The Custom of the Country* is found *Enter the Governour, Clodio, Leopold,
Charino and Attendants at one doore, Hyppolita at the other* (IV);
in *The Queen of Corinth* is found *Enter (at one Doore) Queen,
Theanor, Crates, Conon, Lords, Souldiers (At another) Euphanes
(with two swords) Agenor, Leonidas, Souldiers. . .* (IV.iii). In *The
Changeling* a change of locale is indicated when Alonzo and Deflores
Exeunt at one door & enter at the other (III).

In *The Coxcomb* is found *Enter Pedro and Uberto, severally* (IV);
in *The Queen of Corinth* is found *Enter Neanthes, Sosines, and Eraton,
severally* (I.iii); in *May Day* is found *Enter Lucretia and Temperance
several ways* (II.i) in *The Loyal Subject* are found *Enter Ancient, crying
Broomes, and after him severally, foure Souldiers, crying other things.
Boroskie and Gentleman over the stage observing them* (III.v); and
Enter Gentlemen passing over the stage (IV.i). In *Julius Caesar* is found
Enter Flavius, Murellus, and certaine Commoners over the Stage (IV.i);

in *The Changeling* are found *They pass over in great solemnity* (IV);
Enter Deflores servants: passe over, ring a Bell (V); and *Enter Deflores,
passes over the Stage* (V). In *The Antipodes* is found *A service as
for dinner, pass over the stage, borne by many servitors richly apparel'd,
doing honor to Lefoy as they pass. Exeunt* (I.v); and *These persons
pass over the stage in couples, according as he describes them* (IV.ix).

LARGE PROPERTIES

Banquets, Tables, and Chairs. These are *brought on* or *set forth* in
five plays: *The Launching of the Mary,* "Enter a small banquett, &
wine. musique aloft, after a small respitt of tyme all taken awaye"
(p. 16); "Here bringe a little table, & a paper booke: for Clerke of the
Checke" (p. 50). *Love's Pilgrimage* has *Enter Hostesse and Servants
with Table* (I.i); *Enter Hostesse and Servants with meat* (I.i); *Enter
Leonardo, and Don Zanchio* (*carried by two Servants in a chair*) (II.i);
Enter Roderigo, Markantonio, and a Ship-master. two chairs set out
(II.iii); *The Custom of the Country* has *Banquet set forth* (III.i) and
*Enter Mannuel. Charino. Arnoldo. Zenocia, borne in a chaire. 2 Doctors.
Clodio* (V). *The Loyal Subject* has *Enter two Servants preparing a
Banquet* (IV.v); *The Antipodes* has *Enter in sea gowns and caps, Doctor
and Peregrine brought in a chair by two sailors* (II.iv) and *a table
set forth, covered with treasure* (V.v).

Bar. The Queen of Corinth has *Bar brought in* (V.iv).

Bed. Othello has *Enter Othello, and Desdemona in her bed* (V.ii).
Love's Pilgrimage has *Enter Theodosia and Phillipo on several Beds*
(I.ii); *Cupid's Revenge* has *Enter Hidaspes: Cleophila and Hero,
Hidaspes in a Bedde* (II).

Body. Julius Caesar has *Enter Mark Antony, with Caesars body*
(III.ii.44); *The Custom of the Country* has *Enter Officers and servants
with the body of Duart—Page* (II).

Others. Julius Caesar has *Enter Brutus and goes into the Pulpit, and
Cassius, with the Plebeians* (III.ii). After a picnic scene in *The Launching of the Mary,* a stage direction reads, "enter boye agayne takes bush

& all awaye, perfumes the roome" (p. 86). In *The Loyal Subject* the prompter's warning *Little Trunke ready* is followed by *Enter with the Trunck* (II.v).

Other plays first acted by professionals in the years 1599–1642 and first printed during 1600–1659. Listed in order of first printing.

Every Man out of His Humour (163), Jonson, 1600 (Bodleian). King's men at Court, 8 January 1605 (Chambers, III, 360–363). TP (1600) : "As it was first composed by the Author B. I. *Containing more than hath been publikely Spoken or Acted.*"

Jack Drum's Entertainment (177), Marston?, 1601 (Folger). (Chambers, IV, 21). TP: Paul's boys.

Blurt Master-Constable (188), Middleton?, 1602 (Huntington). (Chambers, III, 439). TP: Paul's boys.

The Parasitaster (230), Marston, 1606 (Pforzheimer). (Chambers, III, 432–433). TP: Queen's Revels at Blackfriars.

Michaelmas Term (244), Middleton, 1607 (Pforzheimer). (Chambers, III, 440). TP: Paul's boys. "There is no clear evidence that the manuscript behind [Q] has been used as a theater prompt book; rather . . . [evidence] suggests that this quarto was set up from Middleton's own draft of the play." Richard Levin, ed. (Lincoln; University of Nebraska Press, 1966), pp. xxii–xxiii.

The Miseries of Enforced Marriage (249), Wilkins, 1607 (Huntington). (Chambers, III, 513). TP: King's men.

Sir Thomas Wyatt (256), Dekker with Webster, and others?, 1607 (Huntington). (Chambers, III, 293–294). TP: Queen Anne's men. "The text clearly being a corrupt memorial reconstruction, there can be no transcriptional link between the autograph papers for the original form of the play and the manuscript furnished to the printer;

hence, what the true original was like we shall never know." Bowers, *Dekker*, I, 399.

The Family of Love (263), Middleton, 1608 (Pforzheimer). (Chambers, III, 440–441). TP: King's Revels.

The Conspiracy and Tragedy of Charles Duke of Byron (274 & 275), Chapman, 1608 (Huntington). (Chambers, III, 257–258). TP: Blackfriars.

May Day (297), Chapman, 1611 (Huntington). (Chambers, III, 256). TP: Blackfriars.

Herod and Antipater (382), Markham, 1622 (Huntington). (Bentley, IV, 734–735). TP: Red Bull (Revels) company.

The Heir (384), May, 1622 (Huntington). (Bentley, IV, 835–837). TP: Red Bull (Revels) company.

The Duke of Milan (386), Massinger, 1623 (Huntington). (Bentley, IV, 775–777). TP: King's men at Blackfriars.

The Bondman (408), Massinger, 1624 (Folger). Revels license for Lady Elizabeth's men, 3 December 1623; Lady Elizabeth's men at Whitehall, 27 December 1623; protected for Beeston's boys, 10 August 1639 (Bentley, IV, 765–770). TP: Lady Elizabeth's men at the Phoenix.

The Roman Actor (424), Massinger, 1629 (Pforzheimer). Revels license for the King's men, 11 October 1626 (Bentley, IV, 815–817). TP: King's men at Blackfriars.

The Just Italian (428), Davenant, 1630 (Huntington). Revels license, 2 October 1629 (Bentley, III, 204–205). TP: King's men at Blackfriars.

The Picture (436), Massinger, 1630 (Huntington). Revels license for the King's men, 8 June 1629 (Bentley, IV, 808–810). TP: King's men at the Globe and Blackfriars.

The Maid of Honour (470), Massinger, 1632 (Huntington). Protected for Beeston's boys, 10 August 1639 (Bentley, IV, 796–799). TP: Queen Henrietta's men at the Phoenix.

Perkin Warbeck (491), Ford, 1634 (Folger). (Bentley, III, 454–456). TP: Queen Henrietta's men at the Phoenix.

The Late Lancashire Witches (494), Richard Brome with Heywood, 1634 (British Museum). Revels Office records, 20 July 1634; Crosfield's *Diary*, 10 July 1635 (Bentley, III, 73–76). TP: King's men at the Globe.

The Great Duke of Florence (505), Massinger, 1636 (Huntington). Revels license for Queen Henrietta's men, 5 July 1627; protected for Beeston's boys, 10 August 1639 (Bentley, IV, 786–788). TP: Queen Henrietta's men at the Phoenix.

Hannibal and Scipio (513), Nabbes, 1637 (Columbia). (Bentley, IV, 934–936). TP: Queen Henrietta's men at the Phoenix.

The Lady's Trial (555), Ford, 1639 (Morgan). Revels license for the Phoenix, 3 May 1638 (Bentley, III, 446–447). TP: Beeston's boys at the Phoenix.

A New Trick To Cheat the Devil (561), Davenport, 1639 (Huntington). Protected for Beeston's boys, 10 August 1639 (Bentley, III, 234–235).

The Prisoners (619), Thomas Killigrew, (collection) 1641 (Huntington). (Bentley, IV, 708–709). TP: Queen Henrietta's men at the Phoenix.

Claricilla (*Claracilla*) (620), Thomas Killigrew, (collection) 1641 (Huntington). (Bentley, IV, 698–700). TP: Queen Henrietta's men at the Phoenix.

The False One (645), Fletcher, with Massinger?, (collection) 1647 (Columbia). Revels Office records, ca. 1619–20 (Bentley, III, 340–342). "It has not been possible to find any directions which suggest, even remotely, the specific influence of the prompter." Bald, *Folio,* pp. 109–110.

Love's Cure (661), Fletcher, with Beaumont?, revised by Massinger?, (collection) 1647 (Columbia). Protected for King's men with variant title, 7 August 1641 (Bentley, III, 363–366).

The Widow (705), Middleton, with Jonson and Fletcher?, 1652 (Pforzheimer). Protected for King's men, 7 August 1641 (Bentley, IV, 900–903). TP: King's men at Blackfriars.

The Court Beggar (720), Richard Brome, (collection) 1653 (Huntington). (Bentley, III, 61–65).

The Cunning Lovers (736), Alexander Brome, 1654 (Columbia). Protected for Beeston's boys, 10 August 1639 (Bentley, III, 48–49). TP: Beeston's boys at the Phoenix.

The Bashful Lover (758), Massinger, (collection) 1655 (Pforzheimer). Revels license for King's men, 9 May 1636; protected for King's men, 7 August 1641 (Bentley, IV, 760–762). TP: King's men at Blackfriars.

ABOVE THE STAGE

A space *above* or *aloft* is referred to in twenty-five plays: *Every Man out of His Humour* (I); *Blurt Master-Constable* (Ev, E2, F2, F3v); *Parasitaster* (V); *Michaelmas Term* (II); *The Miseries of Enforced Marriage* (G2v); *The Family of Love* (III, V); *May Day* (III, IV); *Herod and Antipater* (I); *The Duke of Milan* (II); *The Bondman* (IV.ii); *The Roman Actor* (IV.i); *The Just Italian* (III); *The Picture* (IV.ii, IV.iv); *The Maid of Honour* (II.iv); *Perkin Warbeck* (II.i, III); *The Great Duke of Florence* (II.iii, V.i); *The Lady's Trial* (III); *A New Trick To Cheat the Devil* (III, V); *The Prisoners* (V.ii); *Claricilla* (*Claracilla*) (V); *The False One* (III.iv, V.ii); *Love's Cure* (IV.ii, V.iii); *The Cunning Lovers* (II, III); *The Court Beggar* (III); *The Bashful Lover* (V). This space is referred to as a *window* in seven plays: *Every Man out of His Humour* (I); *Jack Drum's Entertainment* (II); *The Family of Love* (I); *The Heir* (II, V); *The*

Just Italian (IV) ; *Hannibal and Scipio* (I.iii) ; *The Widow* (I). It is called a *casement* in *Jack Drum's Entertainment* (II), and *the walls* in *Sir Thomas Wyatt* (E3). The direction *music above* appears in three plays: *The Conspiracy and Tragedy of Charles Duke of Byron* (II) ; *The Roman Actor* (II.i) : *The Picture* (III.v, IV.iv). An actor *ascends* to the area above in *The Family of Love* (I), and actors *descend* in *The Roman Actor* (IV.ii), *The Picture* (IV.iv), and *Love's Cure* (IV.ii).

ENTRANCES

At one door and . . . at the other or a similar wording is found in eight plays: *Every Man out of His Humour* (L) ; *Jack Drum's Entertainment* (I, III) ; *Herod and Antipater* (I.i, II, III) ; *The Bondman* (V.ii) ; *The Roman Actor* (I.iv) ; *The Just Italian* (III) ; *The Widow* (IV.i) ; *The Bashful Lover* (I.i). *Several doors* or *severally* appears in nine plays: *The Family of Love* (II.i) ; *Herod and Antipater* (I, IV) ; *The Just Italian* (V) ; *The Maid of Honour* (IV.v) ; *The Late Lancashire Witches* (II, III, V) ; *The Lady's Trial* (I) ; *A New Trick To Cheat the Devil* (V.iii) ; *The False One* (V.iv) ; *Love's Cure* (II.iii). *Pass over the stage* or a similar wording is found in five plays: *Every Man out of His Humour* (IV.ii) ; *Blurt Master-Constable* (Bv) ; *Sir Thomas Wyatt* (A4) ; *Claricilla* (*Claracilla*) (V) ; *The Cunning Lovers* (V).

LARGE PROPERTIES

Banquets, Tables, Chairs, and Stools. These are *brought on* or *set forth* in nine plays: *Parasitaster* (II) ; *The Duke of Milan* (I) ; *The Bondman* (II.ii, III.ii) ; *The Roman Actor* (II.i) ; *The Late Lancashire Witches* (IV) ; *The Great Duke of Florence* (IV.ii) ; *A New Trick To Cheat the Devil* (V) ; *The Cunning Lovers* (V) ; *The Court Beggar* (III). Another text does not specify how these properties are introduced: *The Widow* (I.i).

Bar. One is needed in *The Conspiracy and Tragedy of Charles Duke of Byron* (V).

Bed. One is *thrust out* in *The Late Lancashire Witches* (V) and *pulled in* in *A New Trick To Cheat the Devil* (V.iii). A *Couch* is needed in *The Roman Actor* (V) and *The Court Beggar* (II).

Body. One is *brought on* in *The Duke of Milan* (V) and *The False One* (V.iv); and a *Coffin* is called for in *Michaelmas Term* (IV).

Others. A *Canopy* is required in *The Just Italian* (IV), *The Picture* (I.ii), *The Maid of Honour* (IV.ii); a *Carpet* in *The Conspiracy and Tragedy of Charles Duke of Byron* (I); a *Chariot* in *The Bashful Lover* (IV); a *Scaffold* in *Herod and Antipater* (V); a *State* in *Parasitaster* (V), *The Great Duke of Florence* (V); *Stocks* in *Perkin Warbeck* (V); a *Throne* in *Perkin Warbeck* (I.i); a *Tree* in *Parasitaster* (V); a *Trunk* in *The Family of Love* (II, III), *Herod and Antipater* (I).

4 Doors or Hangings

The 102 plays considered in this chapter require movable doors or hangings to cover an accessory stage space where actors can hide, or where actors, large properties, or both can be "discovered." Here "discover" has the sense of "to disclose, or expose to view (anything covered up or previously unseen), to reveal, show." In a few plays stage directions specify that a movable door is closed or locked, or that it is opened to make a discovery; either of the two doors shown in the Swan façade (Plate I) is suited to these actions. Many more plays require concealment by curtains, hangings, or an arras, which are drawn or parted for a discovery. These plays can be performed with the hangings shown in the *Roxana, Messalina,* and *Wits* drawings (Plates II, III, and IV). In Massinger's *The City Madam* there appear notations that are evidently derived from prompt copy: *Whil'st the Act Plays, the Footstep, little Table, and Arras hung up for the Musicians* (IV.iv). Hangings can be fitted over the open doorways of the screens at Hampton Court, the Middle Temple, the Cockpit-in-Court and the Jones/Webb drawings (Plates VI, VII, VIII, and IX), or hung in front of the space below the gallery at Trinity Hall (Plate V). If the doors of the Swan stage are left open, this façade can also be fitted with hangings suitable for the scenes that require them.

It should be remembered that the King's men did not invariably stage the same scene in the same way. In *The Woman's Prize,* for instance, where the Folio text reads *Enter Livia discovered abed, and Moroso by her* (V.i), the manuscript reads "Enter Livia sick carryed in a chaire by servants: Moroso by her." Thus, the actors probably improvised procedures according to the auditorium and stage properties available to them. So, too, when in *The Second Maiden's Tragedy* an actor opens

45

a door and the stage direction states "The Toombe here discovered ritchly set forthe" (p. 55), it should not be assumed that this procedure was followed in all other texts that call for *Tomb discovered* or simply *A Tomb*. In plays where the means of concealment and discovery of the tomb are not specified, one should not rule out alternate possibilities, such as curtains hung from the gallery or a curtained booth set up against the tiring-house façade, as Reynolds and Hodges suggest.[1]

The accessory space is used frequently as a hiding place for one actor who eavesdrops, but it also may be localized temporarily as a *closet*, a *study*, or a *shop*. After actors and properties are discovered in such scenes, however, the action flows to and from the main playing area and the scene ends with the familiar *exeunt*. Since entire scenes are not played within the confines of this space, it should not be thought of as an "inner stage." This is a misleading term of recent coinage that is not used in any pre-Restoration play acted by professionals.[2]

Sometimes *enter* is used as the equivalent of *discovered*. For example, in *The Welsh Embassador* the prompter's warning "bee redy Carintha at a Table" (p. 37) implies that she is already in place at the table within the discovery space before "Enter Carintha at a Table readinge" (p. 38). During a later scene the reminder by the prompter to "sett out a Table" (p. 60) suggests that the table is set in the discovery space to prepare for the next scene, which begins "Enter Clowne in his study writing" (p. 61). So, too, in other plays with "study" scenes, and some others that require large properties, it would be expedient to have the actor in place in the discovery space before the scene starts. Thus, the meanings of *enter* and *discovered* are not mutually exclusive. *Enter* is the more comprehensive of the two terms and may denote *discovered*, whereas *discovered* never describes a conventional walk-on entrance.

Prompt books, manuscripts dependent on prompt copy, and a printed text with manuscript prompter's markings, for plays first acted by professionals in the years 1599–1642. Listed in order of presumed date of first performance.

The Second Maiden's Tragedy (MS), Anonymous (British Museum). License by Sir George Buck, Master of the Revels, at the end of

the text: "This second Maydens tragedy (for it hath no name inscribed) may wth the reformations bee acted publikely. 31 octobr.
1611. G. Buc." (Chambers, IV, 45). "[A] revisional hand has added
a number of stage-directions evidently in the playhouse. They include
mention of two actors: Mr. [Robert] Goughe, who most likely took
the part of Memphonius . . . and Richard Robinson, who played the
Lady. Both are well known as members of the King's company at
the date in question." Greg, *Documents*, I, 265. I cite Greg's edition
of the MS, MSR (London, 1909 [1910]).

The Woman's Prize (MS), Fletcher (Folger). Performance by King's
men suppressed by Master of the Revels, 18 October 1633; allowed,
21 October 1633; at St. James, 28 November 1633 (Adams, *Herbert*,
pp. 20–21, 53; Chambers, III, 222). The Folger MS. and the 1647
Folio text of this play are discussed by Bald, *Folio*, pp. 50–78.

Hengist, King of Kent; or The Mayor of Queenborough (MS), Middleton (Folger). Revels Office records, ca. 1619–20; protected for the
King's men, 7 August 1641 (Bentley, IV, 883–887). I cite the edition
of R. C. Bald, who states: "A dramatic manuscript containing such
clearly marked theatrical cuts and various actors' names in stage-directions would, under normal circumstances, be unhesitatingly pro-
nounced a prompt-book, but here, where the same features appear
in the two manuscripts of the play, and where the manuscripts are
in the hand of the same scribe, both can scarcely be prompt-copies,
and it is probable that neither is. It seems to be more reasonable
to assume that if the scribe was capable of mechanically transcribing
theatrical notes when he made one copy of the play, he was capable
of doing it when he made a second one later. That a prompter's
notes might find their way into a private transcript is proved by another play in the Lambarde volume. The manuscript of Berkeley's
Lost Lady there was apparently made for presentation to Queen Henrietta Maria, but it contains a number of obvious prompter's notes
which have been included by the scribe, but which were deleted by
the author when he corrected the manuscript. The two manuscripts
of *Hengist*, therefore, are probably private transcripts; but there is
little doubt that the scribe's 'copy' was an annotated prompt-book."
Bald, ed., (New York: Charles Scribner's Sons, 1938), pp. xxviii–xxix.

The Honest Man's Fortune (MS), Fletcher, (with Field? Massinger? Tourneur?) (Victoria and Albert Museum). Revels licence for revival by King's men, 8 February 1624; Revels license, without signature, at end of text (Chambers, III, 227). I cite the edition of J. Gerritsen, who states: "Of the two extant versions one, the Dyce manuscript, was copied out by the prompter of the King's Company— now identified with certainty as Edward Knight—and then further prepared, and perhaps used, for prompting at Blackfriars in 1625. The other, the printed text in the Beaumont and Fletcher folio of 1647, seems to have been edited to some extent for the benefit of the reader." Gerritsen, ed. (Groningen, Djakarta: J. B. Wolters, 1952), p. ix. See also, Greg, *Documents,* I, 288–293; Bald, *Folio,* p. 50.

Sir John van Olden Barnavelt (MS), Fletcher, with Massinger? (British Museum). Mentioned in letters, 14 and 27 August 1619 (Bentley, III, 415–417). I cite the edition of W. P. Frijlinck (Amsterdam: H. G. Van Dorssen, 1922). Greg states: "There has . . . been an extensive playhouse revision; and many additional directions, including a number of actors' names, have been supplied in a much rougher hand. . . The more important actors mentioned are all known to have been members of the King's company at the date in question." Greg, *Documents,* I, 269.

The Welsh Embassador (MS), Dekker (Cardiff Public Library). (Bentley, III, 267–268). "The large number of anticipatory stage directions in the Cardiff manuscript indicates that a prompter has prepared the piece for performance, but Dr. Greg points out (*Dramatic Documents,* p. 279) that there is no evidence of actual use as a prompt copy. He notes also that the manuscript—the anticipatory stage directions as well as text—was copied by the same scribe who prepared the Dyce MS. of Massinger's *Parliament of Love.* Since [the latter] play was licensed by Sir Henry Herbert 3 November 1624 for the Cockpit [Phoenix] company, i.e. Lady Elizabeth's men, there is some reason to think *The Welsh Embassador* was of approximately the same date and perhaps prepared for the same company." Bentley, III, 267. "No evidence exists whether, after all the preparation, the manuscript was actually put to use as a prompt-book for a production. There is, of course, no evidence that it was not." Bowers, *Dekker,*

IV, 304. I cite the edition of H. Littledale and W. W. Greg, eds., MSR (London, 1920).

A Game at Chess (MS), Middleton (Folger). King's men at the Globe, 6–15 August 1624. (Bentley, IV, 870–879). "Once owned by the eighteenth century Irish antiquary, Mervyn Archdale, this manuscript (Folger Library: v.a. 231) is dated 13 August 1624, thus in the middle of the play's brief run, and presents what is obviously an early version of the play." J. W. Harper, ed. (London: Benn, 1966), p. xxv. R. C. Bald states that this manuscript is "in all probability the earliest of those which have survived" and notes that "in several places the stage directions of [this] manuscript differ slightly from those in the other texts, and at least two of them throw some light on the way in which the play was produced." Bald, "An Early Version of Middleton's 'A Game at Chesse,' " *MLR,* 38:177, 179(1943). George R. Price describes this text as "a transcript of the promptbook" in his "The Quartos of *The Spanish Gypsy* and Their Relation to *The Changeling.*" *PBSA,* 52:118(1958). I cite the Folger MS., which ends at V.iii, thereby omitting the bag business with which other texts end the play.

Plays first acted by professionals in the years 1599–1642 and first printed during 1600–1659 from prompt copy or texts that may depend wholly or in part on prompt copy. Listed in order of first printing.

The Widow's Tears (301), Chapman, 1612 (Pforzheimer). At Court, 27 February 1613 (Chambers, III, 256–257; Bentley, I, 118). TP: Blackfriars and Whitefriars. "The play was probably printed from the author's holograph, which had been used as a theatrical prompt book. Parrott concurs in this conclusion." Ethel M. Smeak, ed. (Lincoln: University of Nebraska Press, 1966), p. xxv.

Amends for Ladies (356), Field, 1618 (Pforzheimer). (Chambers III, 313–314). TP: Prince Charles's (I) men and Lady Elizabeth's men at Blackfriars. "Four stage directions are confused. . . One speech is wrongly assigned. . . The text contains no serious corruptions.

There is some evidence that the 1618 quarto was printed from a
promptbook." William Peery, ed., *The Plays of Nathan Field* (Austin:
University of Texas Press, 1950), p. 154.

The Cruel Brother (427), Davenant, 1630 (Huntington). Revels license,
12 January 1626/7 (Bentley, III, 201). TP: King's men at Blackfriars.
"Both texts of *The Cruel Brother* have several prompt stage directions,
but the folio text [1673] has been cut somewhat." Bentley, III, 201.

The Mad Lover (637), Fletcher, (collection) 1647 (Columbia). At
Court, 5 January 1616/7; Cockpit-in-Court, 5 November 1630; acted
21 May 1639; protected for King's men, 7 August 1641 (Bentley,
III, 373–376). "A prompter has made insertions in the text [actor's
name]." Bald, *Folio,* p. 103.

The Little French Lawyer (639), Fletcher with Massinger, (collection)
1647 (Columbia). Protected for King's men, 7 August 1641 (Bentley,
III, 356–359. "A single preparatory direction *Wine* occurs about a
dozen lines before the direction *Enter Nurse with wine." Bald, *Folio,*
p. 105.

The Lover's Progress (649), Fletcher, revised by Massinger, (collection)
1647 (Columbia). Revels license for King's men, 6 December 1623;
King's men at Whitehall, 1 January 1623/4; Revels license for revision, 7 May 1634; acted 21 May 1634; protected for King's men,
7 August 1641 (Bentley, III, 359–363). "It will probably be conceded
without difficulty that the stage directions . . . show frequent traces
of the prompter's additions." Bald, *Folio,* p. 107.

The Maid in the Mill (653), Fletcher with William Rowley, (collection)
1647 (Columbia). Revels license for King's men, 29 August 1623;
King's men at Hampton Court, 29 September 1623; at St. James,
1 November 1623; King's men at Whitehall, 26 December 1623;
protected for King's men, 7 August 1641 (Bentley, III, 376–380).
"Anticipatory stage directions." Bald, *Folio,* p. 105.

The Sea Voyage (656), Fletcher, revised by Massinger?, (collection)
1647 (Columbia). Revels license for the Globe, 22 June 1622 (Bentley,
III, 411–414). "Anticipatory stage directions." Bald, *Folio,* p. 105.

The Double Marriage (657), Fletcher, with Massinger?, (collection) 1647 (Columbia). Protected for King's men, 7 August 1641 (Bentley, III, 329–332). "Contains a large number of directions for music, with one or two references to properties which may have been added by a prompter, although there are a number which seem to reveal the author. . . [There is] an anticipatory direction *Boy atop* three lines before his speech, and a later direction *Enter Boy with 3 Cans.*" Bald, *Folio,* pp. 107–108.

The Knight of Malta (659), Fletcher, (collection) 1647 (Columbia). Revels Office records, ca. 1619–20; protected for the King's men, 7 August 1641 (Bentley, III, 351–354). "Anticipatory stage directions." Bald, *Folio,* p. 105.

The Spanish Gypsy (717), Middleton with William Rowley, 1653 (Huntington). Revels license for Lady Elizabeth's men at the Phoenix, 9 July 1623; Lady Elizabeth's men at Whitehall, 5 November 1623; protected for Beeston's boys, 10 August 1639 (Bentley, IV, 892–895). TP: Phoenix and Salisbury Court. "The theater scribe's fair copy made for submitting to the censor and for annotation by the prompter. . . Sound effects are placed in the margin, where the bookholder would observe them easily as he prepared the MS for stage use later." George R. Price, "The Quartos of *The Spanish Gypsy* and Their Relation to *The Changeling*," *PBSA,* 52:118–119(1958).

The Walks of Islington and Hogsdon (*Tricks of Youth*) (773), Jordan, 1657 (Huntington). Revels license, 2 August 1641 (Bentley, IV, 688–690). "This manuscript was probably the prompt copy, since that was the copy which normally bore the license of the Master of the Revels at the end of the play, and it is at that point that the compositor set it up, and in Herbert's normal form." Bentley, IV, 688.

The City Madam (788), Massinger, 1659 (Columbia). Revels license for King's men, 25 May 1632; protected for King's men, 7 August 1641 (Bentley, IV, 771–774). TP: Blackfriars, "Printed for Andrew Pennycuicke, one of the Actors." "Copy for the quarto of *The City Madam* was very clearly a manuscript that had been used as a theatrical promptbook. This is evident from the number of anticipatory stage

directions, wherein properties are readied for use in later scenes . . .
musicians are cued . . . and actors are alerted to prepare themselves
behind the scenes. . . Directions such as these are regularly printed
in the margin of the quarto." Cyrus Hoy, ed. (Lincoln: University
of Nebraska Press, 1964), p. xix.

DOORS

The promptbook of *The Second Maiden's Tragedy* describes the following action: the Tyrant asks two soldiers to bring "the keyes of the
Cathedrall" and "lanthornes and a pickax" (pp. 53–54). One soldier
goes out and returns with the keys; the second promises to bring the
other items. The Tyrant makes his "exit," and the others follow. The
next scene begins with the stage direction "Enter the Tirant agen at
a farder dore, which opened, bringes hym to the Toombe wher the
Lady lies buried: The Toombe here discovered ritchly set forthe" (p.
55). Later in the scene, "On a sodayne in a kinde of Noyse like a
Wynde, the dores clattering, the Toombstone flies open, and a great
light appears in the midst of the Toombe; His Lady as went owt,
standing just before hym all in white, Stuck with Jewells and a great
crucifex on her brest" (p. 61). Since the action requires only one other
entrance later in this scene, a plausible interpretation for this discovery
may be that the Tyrant opens "the farder dore" to reveal the tomb,
which in turn has doors of its own.

Later in this play doors are again given dramatic significance. In
an unlocalized scene Votarius suggests that Anselmus lock himself in
a closet in his wife's chamber so that he may gain proof of her infidelity.
Anselmus and Votarius exit separately. In the next scene Anselmus re-
enters and delivers a brief soliloquy, followed by the prompter's note
"Locks him self in" (p. 64). Anselmus' wife and servant enter; after
their brief conversation, Votarius comes "to the door" and speaks from
"within" (p. 65). The servant admits him, but the wife spurns Votarius'
attentions and Anselmus emerges to confront Votarius. Neither door
is localized in the scene that follows.

The Woman's Prize has "Enter Maria. Servants carrying out household
stuffe & truncks" (III). Other characters enter, and she tells them
she is fleeing the house because her husband Petruchio has "the sick-
nesse." She asks the Watchmen to "lock the doores up fast" and the

stage direction reads "they lock the doore." Petruchio shouts from "within," asking to be let out. After all leave the stage, "Enter Petruchio with a peece, and forces the doore open."

In *The Maid in the Mill* news comes that the King is approaching, whereupon Otrante locks Florimell "in a closet" (V.ii). The King enters, asks to see what is in "this little room," and commands that the lock be forced. Two lines later there is the direction *Florimell discovered,* and she steps forth to play the rest of the scene. In *The Little French Lawyer* Lamira and Anabell are shut up "in a vault" at the end of Act Four; Act Five opens with the direction *Enter one and opens the Chamber doore, in which Lamira and Anabell were shut, they all in feare.*

These stage directions indicate that some plays were acted on a stage with at least one movable door. It should be emphasized, however, that these actions could also be performed without doors. For instance, in *Love's Cruelty* is the direction *Hippolito seemes to open a chamber doore and brings forth Eubella* (IV).

HANGINGS

During a scene in *The Honest Man's Fortune,* the prompter notes "Lamyra showes her Selfe at the Arras" (p. 73); in an aside she says, "I will observe this better." She remains hidden and overhears the conversation of the other characters on stage before the prompter's direction "Ent: Lamyra: from the Aras" (p. 75). Eavesdropping behind the arras also occurs in *The Spanish Gypsy,* where after *Enter Clara, Maria and Pedro from behinde the Arras* (V), Clara reveals that she has overheard Roderigo declare his love for her. In *The Walks of Islington and Hogsdon* occurs the direction *Splendora stands within the Arras* while she overhears Mr. Nice and Mercurio (I). In *The City Madam* the arras is used to conceal musicians who play after they *come down to make ready for the song at Aras* (V.i).

The hangings are also used as a place of concealment in *The Lover's Progress,* in which *Enter Clarinda with a Taper, and Lisander with a Pistole, two Chaires set out* (III.i). At this point there is the prompter's stage direction *Caliste sitting behind a Curtaine.* Clarinda tells Lisander, "I'll leave ye now, draw but that Curtain, And Have your wish," and she makes her *exit.* There are no stage directions here for Lisander, but the dialogue suggests that he draws the curtain and sees Calista asleep in the chair. She awakes, and the two characters play a love scene that is interrupted by *Noise within.* Calista tells him to "retire behind the hangings and there stand close." Her husband Cleander *enters,* and after a brief scene he leaves. Calista then calls forth Lisander, who makes his *exit.*

Two plays that may depend on playhouse copy require curtains for the discovery of actors, or large properties, or both. *Amends for Ladies* has *A Curtain drawne, a bed discover'd Ingen with his sword in his hand, and a Pistoll, the Ladie in a peticoate, the Parson* [sic] (V). This suggests that curtains may be drawn in earlier scenes: *Enter Seldome his wife working as in their shop* (II.i), and *Fee-Simple on a bed, as in Bould's chamber* (III). *The Mad Lover* (V) has the following sequence of stage directions: *Enter Calis and her Traine with lights singing . . .* [song]; *Enter a Nun* [speech]; *Exit Nun and draws the Curten close to Calis. Enter Stremon and Eumenes* [twelve speeches]; *Exeunt Eumenes Stremen Calis* [ready]; *Enter Nun, she opens the Curtain to Calis. Calis at the Oracle, Arras.* The scene ends *Exeunt Calis & Nun.* Some plays mention hangings in the stage directions but do not require them in the action. *The Maid in the Mill* has the preparatory stage direction *Six Chaires placed at the Arras* (II.i), but hangings are not needed in subsequent action. Florimell is *discovered* later in the play, but dialogue suggests that her entrance is preceded by the unlocking of a door (V.ii). *The Cruel Brother* has directions apparently derived from the prompter: *Chaire at the Arras* (II) and *A Chayre at the Arras* (V).

OTHER DISCOVERIES

Eight plays give no indication as to whether discoveries are made by opening a door or by parting curtains. In *A Game at Chess,* The Induction begins "Ignatius discovered and Error a-sleepe," and in Act Five is found "An Altar discovered, richly adorned, and divers Statues standing on each-side." *Hengist* has a dumb show: "ffortune is discovered uppon an alter, in her hand a golden round full of Lotts." (p. 12); *Barnavelt* has "Enter Barnavelt (in his studdy)" (p. 52). *The Double Marriage* has *He discovers Violet and Ascanio in the Bilboes* [shackles] (II). Stage directions in *The Welsh Embassador* call for "Enter Carintha at a Table readinge" (p. 38) and "Enter Clowne in his study writinge"

(p. 61), but the text does not specify how these properties are brought into view.

Also in this play a *tableau vivant* is displayed in the area above. Although curtains are not specified here, it is difficult to see how the *tableau* could be managed without them. A scene between Carintha and the King has a warning for actors inserted in the margin: "bee redy Penda and Voltimar above" (p. 26). Carintha tells the King that she has a "rare picture" to show him; curtains above may be parted to reveal a *tableau* as Carintha "shews Penda with a Leadinge staff voltimar at his back; his sword in him" (p. 27). She explains to the King that she has hired a workman to carve this "statue" of Penda. There is no direct reference to the closing of curtains, but Voltimar is needed for a conventional entrance in the scene following, and the prompter notes marginally "bee redy Chester Cornewall & Voltimar" (p. 27). Curtains in the gallery above are shown in the *Messalina* and *The Wits* drawings. (Plates III and IV.)

In *The Knight of Malta* an apparent prompter's notation, *Discover Tombe,* near the end of IV.i anticipates the use of the tomb in the scene that follows. Miranda, Norandine, and Collona enter a church and hear a groaning "in the wall." They go to the "tomb" and read a "tablet" with a newly inscribed epitaph of Oriana, who soon *rises up* to speak to them. Later in this play is found a prompter's warning *Altar ready, Tapers & booke* (V.i), which anticipates *An Altar discovered, with Tapers, and a Book on it. The two Bishops stand on each side of it. Mountferrat, as the Song is singing ascends up the Altar* (V.ii). *The Sea Voyage* has a note apparently derived from the prompter *An Alter prepar'd* (V). *The Widow's Tears* has *Enter Lysander like a Souldier disguisde at all parts, a halfe Pike, gorget, &c. he discovers the Tombe, lookes in and wonders &c* (IV). In this scene the tombe is open and shut twice; later directions read *Tomb opens, and Lysander within lies along, Cynthia and Ero* (V), and *Shut the Tomb* (V).

ENTRANCES

At one doore and . . . at the other or a similar wording is found in eight plays: *The Honest Man's Fortune,* "Ent: Amiens: At one doore: Montaigne: and Veramour. At Another." (p. 30); *The Woman's Prize,* "Enter Rowland at one doore, Pedro hastly at the other" (I), "Enter Rowland at one doore, Tranio at Ye other" (II); *Hengist,* "Enter

Vortiger Castiza two Ladyes Roxena Devon: Stafford at one Doore
Symon And his Brethren at the other" (p. 59). *The Mad Lover* has
Flourish. *Enter Astorax King of Paphos, his Sister Calis, train and
Cleanthe, Lucippe Gentlewoman at one doore; At the other Eumenes
a Souldier* (I), and *Enter Siphax at one Dore, and a Gentleman at
another* (I); *The Lover's Progress* has *Enter Lidian, Alcidon, (at one
dore) Lisander, Clarange, (at another)* (II); *The City Madam* has
*Lady, Anne, Mary go off at one door; Stargaze and Millisa at the
other* (IV.iv), and *at one door Cerberus, at the other Charon, Orpheus,
Chorus* (V.iii); *The Spanish Gypsy* has *Exit at one door. Enter presently
at the other* (V). *The Cruel Brother* has *Enter Sutors at the other
doore* (I) and *Exit the other way* (V).

The terms *severall* or *severally* are found in nine plays. *The Honest
Man's Fortune* has "Orleans: and Amiens at Severall doores" (p. 7).
The Woman's Prize has "Enter 3 Country wenches at severall doors"
(II). *Barnavelt* has "Enter 2. Captaines: & yeir Soldiers, severally mr.
Rob: mr Rice" (p. 77). *The Lover's Progress* has *Enter Dorilaus, and
Cleander severally* (II), *Enter Alcidon and Beronte severally* (IV), and
*Enter Dorilaus, Caliste, Olinda, Beronte, Alcidon, Servants and Clarinda
at severall doores* (IV). *The Little French Lawyer* has *Exeunt severally*
(II, IV). *The Sea Voyage* has *Enter severally, Lamure, Franvile, Morllat*
(III), *Enter Albert, Aminta, Raymond, Lamure, Morillat, Frankvile,
severally* (V), and *Enter severally, Raymond, Albert Aminta* (V). *The
Double Marriage* has *Enter Citizens severally,* and *Enter 2 Citizens at
both dores, saluting afar off* (III). *The Cruel Brother* has *Exeunt Severall wayes* (III, IV) and *Enter Castruchio, Lothario, Cossimo, severall
wayes* (V). *The Knight of Malta* has *Enter severally Gomera, and Miranda* (II.v).

Pass over the stage or a similar wording is found in seven plays.
The Second Maiden's Tragedy has "Enter Bellarius—passing over the
Stage (p. 30). *Barnavelt* has "Enter ye Arminians: pass over" (p. 27).
The Mad Lover has *Enter Siphax walkes softly over the Stage and
goes in* (V). *The Spanish Gypsy* has *Enter Fernando, Francisco, Pedro,
Roderigo, Clara, Maria, as from Church over the stage, Fernando stayes
Roderigo* (V). *The Little French Lawyer* has *Enter Nurse and Charloth
pass ore the stage with pillowes night Cloaths and such things* (III),
and *Enter foure over the stage with Beaupre and Verdoone bound and
halters about their necks* (V). In *The Double Marriage* Castruchio

comments about other characters as *these pass o're* (I), and *Enter Virolet, Ronvero, Ascanio, and Martia, Passing over* (III). *The Widow's Tears* has *Enter Argus barehead, with whome another Usher Lycus joynes, going over the Stage* (I).

LARGE PROPERTIES

Banquets, Tables, and Chairs. These are *brought on* or *set forth* in eleven plays: *Hengist*, "Hoboys the King and his traine mett by Hengist and Horsus they salute & Exeunt; while the Banquet is Brought forth Musique plays, Enter Vertiger: Horsus, Devon Stafford Castiza Roxena and two Ladies" (p. 60), "then is brought in ye Bodye of Vortiner in a Chaire dead" (p. 69); *The Second Maiden's Tragedy*, "They bringe the Body in a Chaire drest up in black velvet" (p. 70); *The Woman's Prize*, "Enter Livia sick carryed in a chaire by servants: Moroso by her" (V); *The Honest Man's Fortune*, "Enter foure serving in a Banquet" (p. 108). *Barnavelt* has prompter's warnings "Table: Bell" (p. 33) and "Taper: pen & inke Table" (p. 45). *The Knight of Malta* carries the prompter's note *A Table out, two stools* (III.iv).

The Lover's Progress has *Enter Dorilaus, Cleander, Chamberlaine, Table, Tapers, and three stooles* (III). *The Sea Voyage* has *A Table furnisht* (V). *The Cruel Brother* has an anticipatory direction *Chaire out* (II). *The Spanish Gypsy* has *Clara in a Chaire, Pedro and Maria by her* (III). *The City Madam* has *A Table Count book, Standish, Chair and stools set out* (I.ii) and *A chair set out* (II.i). Also in this play, *The banquet ready. One Chair, and Wine* (V.i) anticipates *A table, and rich Banquet* (V.iii).

Bar. Barnavelt carries the prompter's note "A Bar brought in" (p. 60). In *The Lover's Progress* is found *a bar set forth* (V).

Bed. Barnavelt carries the prompter's note "Son abed" (p. 46). In *The Cruel Brother* is found *The Duke (on his Bed) is drawne forth* (V).

Coffin or Hearse. The Woman's Prize calls for "Enter Sophocles, Moroso, Petruchio in a Coffin, carried by Servants" (V). *Barnavelt* needs "a Coffin" (p. 78). *The Mad Lover* has *The Hearse ready Polidor,*

Eumens & Captains (V). *The Double Marriage* has *Enter Pandulf, the Bodies of Virolet, and Juliana, upon a Hearse* (V).

Others. The Woman's Prize requires "Enter Jaques & Pedro Porters with trunke and Hampers" (V). *A Game at Chess* needs "A Litter" (V.i). *Barnavelt* needs "Bowghs & flowres" (p. 58), "A Gibbett" (p. 78), and "A Scaffold put out" (p. 79). *The Double Marriage* has *Enter Ronvere, guard, Executioners with a Rack* (I).

ABOVE THE STAGE

The function of this space as an observation post is described in the dialogue of *The Second Maiden's Tragedy,* where a scene opens with the direction "Leonella above in a Gallery with her love Bellarius" (p. 63). Her following speech may allude to the Lords' room:

> thow knowst this gallerie well tis at thy use now
> t'as bin at myne full often, thow mayst sitt
> like a most privat gallant in y'on corner
> see all the plaie and nere be seene thy self.

After a brief scene above, "Descendet Leonella." Bellarius then observes below him an eight-line soliloquy by Anselmus who "Locks him self in." Soon the wife of Anselmus enters with Leonella (p. 64).

Hengist has the direction "Enter Aurelius and Uther with Souldiers" (p. 90); Uther speaks of a fortified castle, and as he mentions the "murderer of our brother," the prompter notes "Vortiger [and] Horsus on ye walls" (p. 90). Uther says to Aurelius, "There he appeares agen; behold my Lord." Vortiger apparently notices the soldiers and says that he is "Begirt all round" (p. 91). Aurelius and Uther remain below and watch as Vortiger and Horsus above stab each other, then are joined by Roxena (p. 94), whom they also both stab. All three characters above die, and Aurelius comments, "Our peace is full now In yond usurpers fall" (p. 97). At this point Hengist enters, and the dialogue suggests that he laments over the body of Roxena. If so, when she dies, she probably falls from the acting space above onto the main stage. A late printed text (1661) has *She falls* (K2).

Barnavelt requires an acting area above in two scenes. In the first, the Prince of Orange and his followers enter and are greeted by a Captain; the prompter notes in the margin "Enter Capn on ye walls" (p. 25). After a brief exchange between the Captain and those below, the scene ends with "exeunt." Later in the play, Burghers engaged in "merry song" are joined in their celebrations, "Enter wife, above" (p. 59). She has three brief speeches in this unlocalized area before the scene ends with "exeunt."

The space above is also required in twelve other texts that may depend on playhouse copy, including *A Game at Chess*, "Lowd Musick Enter Black King: Queene Duke & Pawnes . . . & Black Bishops Pawn above entertaines them with this Lattin Oration" (V.i); *The Woman's Prize*, "Enter Maria and Bianca above" (I, II), "Musique above" (II), "Enter Livia above" (II), and "Enter above, Maria, Bianca, a Citty wife, a Country wife and 3 women" (II). *The Sea Voyage* has *Aminta above* (I) and a direction for Albert to *Exit and Enter above* (II). *The Knight of Malta* has *Enter (above) Oriana, Zanthia, two Gentlewomen, (beneath) Valetta, Mountferrat, Astorius, Castorot, Gomera, Miranda, Attendants of Knights &c* (I.iii) and *Corporall and Watch above singing* (III.i); *The Mad Lover* has *Enter Memnon above* (II); and *Venus descends* and *Venus ascends* (V). *The Widow's Tears* has *Hymen descends* (III).

The Little French Lawyer has *Enter Cleremont above* (III), and *Lights above, two Servants and Anabell* (III). *The Maid in the Mill* has *Enter Ismena and Aminta above with a Taper* (I.iii), *Enter Aminta (above) with a Taper* (IV.iii), and *Enter Aminta above, and Martin return'd again, ascends* (IV.iii). The space above is used for a *tableau vivant* in *The Welsh Embassador* (p. 27). *The City Madam* has *Musicians come down to make ready for the song at Aras* (V.i). *The Cruel Brother* has *Musicke above* (V). *The Double Marriage* has *Enter Duke of Sesse above and his daughter Martia like an Amazon* (II), and the prompter's warning *Boy atop* followed two lines later by a short speech from *Boy above* (II). This play also has *Enter Ascanio and Martia above* (V), *Enter Ascanio above* (V), and *Enter Ferrand, Martia, Ascanio, and Ronvere, above* (V).

Other plays first acted by professionals in the years 1599–1642 and first printed during 1600–1659. Listed in order of first printing

Henry the Fifth (165), Shakespeare, (collection) 1623 (Columbia). King's men at Whitehall, 7 January 1604/5 (Chambers, *WS*, I,

388–396; II, 331). "Dover Wilson, whose [Cambridge] edition of the play appeared in 1947, rejecting earlier speculations, concurs in the 'fairly general agreement' that Q[1600] is a reported text. . . It is encouraging to find that he recognizes F as having been printed from Shakespeare's foul papers." Greg, *Folio,* pp. 282, 285.

The Shoemakers' Holiday (175), Dekker, 1600 (Folger). (Chambers, III, 291–292). TP: Admiral's men at Court, 1 January 1599/1600. "There are no definite signs of theatrical, or prompt, copy, and some indication that the author's papers may have been used, possibly the 'foul papers,' although a transcript of these cannot be ruled out of the question." Bowers, *Dekker,* I, 9.

The Merry Wives of Windsor (*Sir John Falstaff*) (187), Shakespeare, 1602 (Huntington). King's men at Whitehall, 4 November 1604; King's men at the Cockpit-in-Court, 15 November 1638 (Chambers, *WS,* II, 331, 353). TP: Chamberlain's men "before her Majestie, and else-where." "[Quarto] is clearly a reported text, apparently a memorial reconstruction of a version closely allied to, if not substantially identical with, F . . . [which text] has the peculiarity that each scene is headed by an entrance for all the characters that appear in it, irrespective of whether they enter at the beginning or later on, that similarly the only exits are at the ends of scenes, and that there are no other stage-directions. . . The absence of stage directions deprives us of what is usually our chief ground of judgement [about printer's copy]." Greg, *Folio,* pp. 334–336.

Thomas Lord Cromwell (189), Anonymous, 1602 (Folger). (Chambers, IV, 8). TP: Chamberlain's men.

How a Man May Choose a Good Wife from a Bad (191), Anonymous, 1602 (British Museum). (Chambers, IV, 19–20). TP: Worcester's men.

Satiromastix (195), Dekker, with Marston?, 1602 (Huntington). (Chambers, III, 293). TP: Chamberlain's men and Paul's boys. "The exact nature of the printer's copy is not certain, but there seems to be no indication of any link with a prompt-book. Dekker's preface and his errata list show that the text was authorized; but whether the copy was 'foul papers' or a transcript of these papers cannot be demonstrated." Bowers, *Dekker,* I, 301.

1 The Honest Whore (*The Converted Courtesan*) (204), Dekker with Middleton, 1604 (Huntington). Prince Henry's men ca. 1604 (Chambers, III, 294–295). "The printer's copy was foul papers or a transcript from them. There are no certain signs of prompt-book origin, and the only two possible hints are both suspect." Bowers, *Dekker,* II, 3–4.

1 If You Know Not Me You Know Nobody (215), Heywood, 1605 (Pforzheimer). (Chambers, III, 342–343). "Its text is interesting as the only extant Elizabethan play which is stated by an authoritative contemporary witness—the author himself—to have been reported by stenography. . . The text as we have it was put together and reconstructed by the actors who played the 'good' characters [those whose verse is regular metrically]. This hypothesis would also account for the fact that the exceptions to the 'badness' of the other characters occur when the good characters are present on the stage, taking part in the dialogue, or just above to enter, when the actor would be listening intently for his cue." G. N. Giordano-Orsini, "Thomas Heywood's Play on 'The Troubles of Queen Elizabeth,'" *Library,* 4th ser. XIV: 313, 321 (1934).

2 If You Know Not Me You Know Nobody (*2 Queen Elizabeth's Troubles* (224), Heywood, 1606 (Huntington). (Chambers, III, 342–343).

Sir Giles Goosecap (228), Chapman?, 1606 (Pforzheimer). (Chambers, IV, 15–16). TP: Chapel Children.

The Woman Hater (245), Beaumont with Fletcher?, 1607 (Huntington). (Chambers, III, 219–220). TP: Paul's boys.

The Puritan (251), Anonymous, 1607 (New York Public Library). (Chambers, IV, 41–42). TP: Paul's boys.

The Revenger's Tragedy (253), Tourner? Middleton?, 1607 (Huntington). (Chambers, IV, 42). TP: King's men. "The stage-directions are inadequate for a performance in the theatre, since many entrances and exits are not given in Quarto." R. A. Foakes, ed. (London: Methuen, 1966), p. lxii.

The Fleer (255), Sharpham, 1607 (Huntington). (Chambers, III, 490–491). TP: Queen's Revels at Blackfriars.

Westward Ho (257), Dekker with Webster, 1607 (Folger). (Chambers, III, 295). TP: Paul's boys. "The manuscript brought to be registered could not have come from the theatre. . . All that is evident is that the printed quarto was set from 'foul papers,' presumably without transcriptional link." Bowers, *Dekker*, II, 313, 314.

A Woman Killed with Kindness (258), Heywood, 1607 (British Museum). (Chambers, III, 341–342). "Though there is no wholly convincing evidence, it seems likely that the manuscript or manuscripts [behind the Quarto] were author's foul papers or a transcript thereof rather than theatrical prompt copy." R. W. Van Fossen, ed. (Cambridge: Harvard University Press, 1961), p. lxvi.

Volpone (259), Jonson, (collection) 1616 (Huntington). (Chambers, III, 368–369). TP: Acted by King's men in 1605. "[Jonson] corrected the proofs of the Folio, but the changes he made in *Volpone* are relatively minor, chiefly involving spelling and punctuation." Alvin B. Kernan, ed. (New Haven: Yale University Press, 1962), p. 229.

The Merry Devil of Edmonton (264), Anonymous, 1608 (Huntington). King's men at Court, 3 May 1618, 15 February 1630/1, and 6 November 1638 (Bentley, I, 133). TP: King's men at the Globe. "[William Amos Abrams] envisages cutting for a provincial tour. There are a few possible dislocations and duplications and a few facile corruptions and vapid phrases that might point to reporting; but they do not amount to much, and the suggestion is hardly borne out by the general character of the text. According to [Abrams] 'the imperative form of certain stage directions seems to suggest a prompter's manuscript' . . . but this evidence is equivocal and the suggestion must certainly be rejected, for prompt copy could not possibly have produced the confusion in the speakers' names that characterizes the

quarto." W. W. Greg, *"The Merry Devil of Edmonton," Library,*
4th ser. 25:129–130(1945).

Law Tricks (267), Day, with Wilkins?, 1608 (Huntington). (Chambers,
III, 285–286). TP: King's Revels. "Though badly printed, the text
is a sound one, and, since it bears no signs of prompt-book origin,
it may have been set up from autograph foul papers." John Crow,
ed. MSR (London, 1949 [1950]), p. v.

Humour out of Breath (268), Day, 1608 (Pforzheimer). (Chambers,
III, 287). TP: King's Revels.

The Rape of Lucrece (273), Heywood, 1608 (Huntington). King's and
Queen's men together at Court, 13 January 1612; at the Phoenix,
August 1628; protected for Beeston's boys, 10 August 1639 (Chambers,
III, 343–344; Bentley, I, 253, 339). TP: Queen Anne's men at the
Red Bull.

A Mad World My Masters (276), Middleton, 1608 (Pforzheimer).
Chambers, III, 439–440). TP (1608): Paul's boys; (1640): Queen's
men at Salisbury Court. "Printer's copy was doubtless a Middleton
holograph, and more than likely the foul papers of the play." Standish
Henning, ed. (Lincoln: University of Nebraska Press, 1965), p. xvii.

The Dumb Knight (277), Markham with Machin?, 1608 (Folger).
(Chambers, III, 418). TP: King's Revels.

Troilus and Cressida (*Troilus and Cresseid*) (279), Shakespeare, 1609
(Huntington). (Chambers, *WS,* I, 438–449). TP: King's men at the
Globe. "Q from a private transcript by the author: F from Q collated
with foul papers." Greg, *Folio,* p. 427.

Pericles (284), Shakespeare, 1609 (Huntington). London, 1608?; King's
men at Whitehall, 20 May 1619; the Globe, 10 June 1631 (Chambers,
WS, II, 335, 346, 348). TP: King's men at the Globe. "If *Pericles*
was indeed wholly Shakespeare's, we should be forced to suppose
that its exclusion from the First Folio was due to the editors' inability
to replace the 'bad' text [1609] by a good one." Greg, *Folio,* p. 98.

The Turk (*Muleasses the Turk*) (286), Mason, 1610 (Huntington). (Chambers, III, 435). TP: King's Revels company.

Ram Alley (292), Barry, 1611 (Huntington). (Chambers, III, 215). TP: King's Revels company.

A Woman Is a Weathercock (299), Field, 1612 (British Museum). (Chambers, III, 313). TP: Queen's Revels company at Whitehall and Whitefriars. "A number of the stage directions seem to be descriptive of a well directed performance; but since the author was also a leading performer, this fact may be of small weight in determining the nature of the copy." William Peery, ed., *The Plays of Nathan Field* (Austin: University of Texas Press, 1950), p. 63.

The Alchemist (303), Jonson, (collection) 1616 (Huntington). King's men at Court, 1612–13; King's men at Whitehall, 1 January 1622/3; King's men, 1 December 1631; revived, January 1638/9 and 18 May 1639 (Chambers, III, 371–372; Bentley, I, 121).

Epicene (*The Silent Woman*) (304), Jonson, (collection) 1616 (Huntington). King's men at St. James, 18 February 1635/6; King's men at the Cockpit-in-Court, 1636 (Adams, *Herbert*, pp. 55, 75; Chambers, III, 369–371). TP: Revels company.

The White Devil (*Vittoria Corombona*) (306), Webster, 1612 (British Museum). (Chambers, III, 509–510). TP: Queen Anne's men. "As a whole, the evidence leads to the conclusion that *The White Devil* was printed from a non-theatrical manuscript which was probably in the author's possession. This manuscript was fair with regard to the spoken word, but among the stage directions and speech directions there were marks of an author's foul papers." J. R. Brown, "The Printing of John Webster's Plays (I)," *SB*, 6:128(1953).

The Insatiate Countess (315), Marston, 1613 (Pforzheimer).(Chambers, III, 433–434). TP: Whitefriars.

Greene's Tu Quoque (323), Cooke, 1614 (Huntington). Queen Anne's men at Court, 27 December 1611 and 2 February 1612; Lady Elizabeth's men at Whitehall, 6 January 1624/5 (Chambers, III, 269–270; Adams, *Herbert,* p. 52). TP: Queen Anne's men.

The Honest Lawyer (337), Anonymous, 1616 (Bodleian). (Chambers, IV, 19). TP: Queen Anne's men.

Philaster (363), Beaumont and Fletcher, Q2, 1620 (Huntington). At Court, winter of 1612–13; payment, 20 May 1613; Revels Office records, ca. 1619–20; King's men at Court, 14 December 1630; King's men at St. James, 21 February 1636/7 (Chambers, III, 222–223; Adams, *Herbert,* p. 58; Bentley, I, 113). "It seems unlikely that any prompt-book, even a provincial one, would contain Q1's kind of verbal inaccuracy and mislineation, to say nothing of the awkwardness in performance that occasionally would have resulted from obeying the Q1 stage directions. . . . [the printer appears to have] set Q2 from an annotated exemplum of the earlier edition . . . The annotator . . . had at his disposal either the prompt-book or authorial fair copy or a transcript of one of them." Robert K. Turner, ed., in Bowers, *B & F,* I, 389, 378, 380.

The Two Merry Milkmaids (364), "I. C.," 1620 (Pforzheimer). At Court, Christmas season of 1619 (Bentley, III, 101–104). TP: Revels company at Court.

The Devil's Law Case (388), Webster, 1623 (Folger). (Bentley, V, 1250–1252). TP: Queen Anne's men.

The Winter's Tale (397), Shakespeare, (collection) 1623 (Columbia). King's men at the Globe, 15 May 1611; King's men, 5 November 1611; King's men at Court, 7 April 1618; Revels Office records, ca. 1619–20; Revels license for revival: "For the king's players. An olde playe called Winter's Tale, formerly allowed of by Sir George Bucke, and likewyse by mee on Mr Hemmings his worde that there was nothing profane added or reformed, thogh the allowed booke was missinge; and therefore I returned it without a fee, this 19 of August, 1623"; King's men at Whitehall, 18 January 1623/4; King's men at Court, 16 January 1633/4 (Chambers, *WS,* II, 340–341, 342, 346, 347, 352). "The prompt-copy must have been in existence at

the time of the court performances of 1618 and 1619, but may possibly
have gone astray on the latter occasion. That would normally, on
the view here taken throughout, have left the company in possession
of the foul papers, which they might have been expected to hand
over to the printer, as they appear to have done in so many other
cases. But if this was the only manuscript of the play they possessed
they may have hesitated to part with it and have preferred to commis-
sion Crane to prepare a transcript on literary lines for use in the
Folio. . . That transcript, however, even if the printer returned it,
would have been of no use on the stage, and when the players were
required to give another court performance they presumably had their
book-keeper prepare a fresh prompt-copy from the foul papers and
persuaded Herbert to license it in the summer of 1623." Greg, *Folio,*
pp. 416–417. In his discussion of the Padua *The Winter's Tale,* Evans
states that this text "represents an unfinished cutting of the play,
one which could never have reached production, [therefore] only two
pages have been reproduced in the facsimile." G. Blakemore Evans,
Shakespearean Prompt-Books of the Seventeenth Century (Charlottesville: Bibliographical Society of the University of Virginia, 1963), II,
part i, 33. For this reason I cite the uncut Columbia text of 1623 *The
Winter's Tale.*

Henry the Eighth (400), Shakespeare, (collection) 1623 (Columbia).
King's men at the Globe, 29 June 1613 (Chambers, *WS,* II, 343–344).
"The copy for F was clearly a carefully prepared manuscript, in whose
hand or hands there is no evidence to show. It could have been used
as a prompt-book, but there is no indication that it was." Greg, *Folio,*
p. 425. "Greg's statement on the play may be modified to this extent;
that the copy for the Folio *Henry VIII* was a carefully prepared
manuscript, probably in a single hand; there is no indication that
it was used as a prompt-book, whereas there is evidence from variations
in speech-headings and the confusion these might occasion in the
theatre, to suggest that it was based on foul papers." R. A. Foakes,
"On the First Folio Text of *Henry VIII," SB,* 11:60(1958).

The Lovers' Melancholy (420), Ford, 1629 (Pforzheimer). Revels license
for Blackfriars, 24 November 1628 (Bentley, III, 448–451). TP: King's
men at Blackfriars and the Globe.

The Grateful Servant (429), J. Shirley, 1630 (Huntington). Revels license, 3 November 1629; protected for Beeston's boys, 10 August 1639 (Bentley, V, 1114–1118). TP: Queen Henrietta's men at the Phoenix.

A Chaste Maid in Cheapside (433), Middleton, 1630 (Pforzheimer). (Chambers, III, 441). TP: Lady Elizabeth's men at the Swan.

Match Me in London, Dekker (440), 1631 (Pforzheimer). Revels license as "an Old Playe," for Lady Elizabeth's men at the Phoenix, 21 August 1623 (Chambers, III, 297–298; Bentley, III, 256). TP: Red Bull and the Phoenix. "Since Dekker signed the dedication to Lodowick Carlell, he doubtless furnished the printer with the manuscript in this case, and indeed the print shows no clear sign of stage influence." Bowers, *Dekker,* III, 253.

The Staple of News (456), Jonson, (collection) 1631 (New York Public Library). (Bentley, IV, 628–632). TP: King's men.

The Emperor of the East (459), Massinger, 1632 (Pforzheimer). Revels license for King's men, 11 March 1630/1 (Bentley, IV, 777–781). TP: King's men at the Globe and Blackfriars.

The Northern Lass (463), Brome, 1632 (Huntington). Revels license for King's men, 29 July 1629 (Bentley, III, 81–84). TP: King's men at the Globe and Blackfriars.

The Fatal Dowry (464), Massinger with Field, 1632 (Pforzheimer). King's men at Court, bill, 3 February 1630/1 (Bentley, IV, 783–785). TP: King's men at Blackfriars.

All's Lost by Lust (471), William Rowley, 1633 (Columbia). Revels Office records, ca. 1619–20; protected for Beeston's boys, 10 August 1639 (Bentley, V, 1018–1021). TP: Lady Elizabeth's men and Queen Henrietta's men at the Phoenix.

Love's Sacrifice (478), Ford, 1633 (Huntington). Protected for Beeston's boys, 10 August 1639 (Bentley, III, 451–453). TP: Queen Henrietta's men at the Phoenix.

The Bird in a Cage (479), James Shirley, 1633 (Folger). Revels license (alternate title), 21 January 1632/3 (Bentley, V, 1080–1081). TP: The Phoenix.

The Broken Heart (480), Ford, 1633 (Library of Congress). (Bentley, III, 439–442). TP: King's men at Blackfriars.

The English Traveller (484), Heywood, 1633 (Huntington). (Bentley, IV, 565–567). TP: Queen Henrietta's men at the Phoenix.

'Tis Pity She's a Whore (486), Ford, 1633 (Morgan). Protected for Beeston's boys, 10 August 1639 (Bentley, III, 462–464). TP: Queen Henrietta's men at the Phoenix.

The Traitor (498), James Shirley, 1635 (Huntington). Revels license, 4 May 1631; protected for Beeston's boys, 10 August 1639 (Bentley, V, 1150–1153). TP: Queen Henrietta's men.

The Platonic Lovers (506), Davenant, 1636 (Folger). Revels license, 16 November 1635 (Bentley, III, 211–212). TP: King's men at Blackfriars.

The Wits (507), Davenant, 1636 (Huntington). Revels license, 9 January 1633/4; at Court, 28 January 1633/34 (Bentley, III, 222–225). TP: King's men at Blackfriars.

The Lady of Pleasure (518), James Shirley, 1637 (Columbia). Revels license, 15 October 1635; at the Phoenix, 5 or 6 November 1635; at the Phoenix, 8 December 1635; protected for Beeston's boys, 10 August 1639 (Bentley, V, 1125–1127). TP: Queen Henrietta's men at the Phoenix.

The Example (521), James Shirley, 1637 (Columbia). Revels license, 24 June 1634; protected for Beeston's boys, 10 August 1639 (Bentley, V, 1108–1110). TP: Queen Henrietta's men at the Phoenix.

The Duke's Mistress (536), James Shirley, 1638 (New York Public Library). Revels license, 18 January 1635/6 (Bentley, V, 1107–1108). TP: Queen Henrietta's men at the Phoenix.

Monsieur Thomas (*Father's Own Son*) (558), Fletcher, 1639 (Morgan). Protected for Beeston's boys, 10 August 1639 (Chambers, III, 228). TP: Blackfriars.

The Unnatural Combat (559), Massinger, 1639 (Pforzheimer). (Bentley, IV, 821–824). TP: King's men at the Globe.

The Maid's Revenge (562), James Shirley, 1639 (Bodleian). Revels license, 9 February 1625/6; protected for Beeston's boys, 10 August 1639 Bentley, V, 1134–1137). TP: Queen Henrietta's men at the Phoenix.

The City Match (568), Mayne, 1639 (Pforzheimer). (Bentley, IV, 847–850). TP: King's men at Whitehall and Blackfriars.

The Opportunity (575), James Shirley, 1640 (Folger). Revels license, 29 November 1634; protected for Beeston's boys, 10 August 1639 Bentley, V, 1134–1137). TP: Queen Henrietta's men at the Phoenix.

The Noble Stranger (597), Sharpe, 1640 (Pforzheimer). (Bentley, V, 1051–1052). TP: Queen Henrietta's men at Salisbury Court.

A Tale of a Tub (617), Jonson, (collection) 1641 (Pforzheimer). License after censorship by Master of the Revels, 7 May 1633; Queen Henrietta's men at Court, 14 January 1633/4 (Bentley, IV, 632–636). "An analysis of the play seems to indicate that In-and-In Medlay was in the play before Vitruvius Hoop was removed and that Jonson has altered the role in the latter half of the play by adding satire on [Inigo] Jones which was not originally intended. Could Herbert have missed the new satire because it was assigned to a character inoffensive in the original version he had read? Even if he did, the theatre audience surely noticed it, and Jones must have heard of it. It is conceivable that the play was performed at the Cockpit [Phoenix] and at Court with Vitruvius Hoop and the motion of a tub eliminated and no further changes, but that Jonson made further alterations in the play to ease his spleen against Jones and that these were published after his death though they had never been acted." Bentley, IV, 635.

Brennoralt (*The Discontented Colonel*) (621), Suckling, 1642 (Harvard). Protected for King's men, 7 August 1641 (Bentley, V, 1207–1209). TP: 1646—King's men at Blackfriars.

The Unfortunate Lovers (624), Davenant, 1643 (Huntington). Revels license, 16 April 1638; King's men at Blackfriars, 23 April 1638; King's men at the Cockpit-in-Court, 31 May 1638; King's men at Hampton Court, 30 September 1638; protected for King's men, 7 August 1641 (Bentley, III, 220–222). TP: King's men at Blackfriars.

The Goblins (628), Suckling, (collection) 1646 (Pforzheimer). Protected for King's men, 7 August 1641 (Bentley, V, 1210–1212). TP: King's men at Blackfriars.

The Noble Gentleman (641), Fletcher, (collection) 1647 (Columbia). Revels license for Blackfriars, 3 February 1625/6; protected for King's men, 7 August 1641 (Bentley, III, 387–391). "It has not been possible to find any directions which suggest, even remotely, the specific influence of the prompter." Bald, *Folio*, 109–110.

The Captain (642), Fletcher, (collection) 1647 (Columbia). King's men at Court, 1612–13 (Chambers, III, 226). "It has not been possible to find any directions which suggest, even remotely, the specific influence of the prompter." Bald, *Folio*, pp. 109–110.

The Pilgrim (658), Fletcher, (collection) 1647 (Columbia). At Court, 1 January 1621/2; at Court 29 December 1622; protected for King's men, 7 August 1641 (Bentley, III, 391–394). "It has not been possible to find any directions which suggest, even remotely, the specific influence of the prompter." Bald, *Folio*, pp. 109–110.

A Jovial Crew [*or the Merry Beggars*] (708), Richard Brome, 1652 (Folger). (Bentley, III, 70–73). TP: Acted at the Phoenix, 1641. "It is reasonably certain that the manuscript behind the 1652 quarto was prepared for publication by the author. . . The many descriptive stage directions . . . seem designed to accommodate the reader rather than the theater." Ann Haaker, ed. (Lincoln: University of Nebraska Press, 1968), p. xxi.

A Mad Couple Well Matched (718), Richard Brome (collection) 1653 (Pforzheimer). Protected for Beeston's boys, 10 August 1639 (Bentley, III, 80–81).

The Novella (719), Richard Brome, (collection) 1653 (Pforzheimer). Protected for King's men, 7 August 1641 (Bentley, III, 84–85). TP: King's men at Blackfriars, 1632.

The Imposture (726), James Shirley, (collection) 1653 (Columbia). Revels license, 10 November 1640; protected for King's men, 7 August 1641 (Bentley, V, 1123–1125). TP: Blackfriars.

The Cardinal (727), James Shirley, (collection) 1653 (Columbia). Revels license, 25 November 1641 (Bentley, V, 1084–1088). TP: Blackfriars. "The manuscript given to [the printer] was either the author's own copy or a careful transcript of the author's copy made for uses other than theatrical production." Charles R. Forker, ed. (Bloomington: Indiana University Press, 1964), p. xxvi.

The Gentleman of Venice (747), James Shirley, 1655 (Huntington). Revels license, 30 October 1639 (Bentley, V, 1112–1114). TP: Queen Henrietta's men at Salisbury Court.

King John and Matilda (749), Davenport, 1635 (Huntington). Protected for Beeston's boys, 10 August 1639 (Bentley, III, 232–234). TP: Queen Henrietta's men at the Phoenix.

The Guardian (759), Massinger, (collection) 1655 (Pforzheimer). Revels license for King's men, 31 October 1633; King's men at Court, 12 January 1633/4; protected for King's men, 7 August 1641 (Bentley, IV, 789–790). TP: King's men at Blackfriars.

More Dissemblers besides Women (781), Middleton, (collection) 1657 (Huntington). Revels license as "An Old Play," 17 October 1623; King's men at Whitehall, 6 January 1623/4; protected for King's men, 7 August 1641 (Bentley, IV, 888–889).

The Weeding of the Covent Garden (808), Richard Brome, (collection) 1659 (Huntington). (Bentley, III, 89–92).

In *The Merry Wives of Windsor* Mistress Quickly *opens the doore* (I.iv.43) to admit Doctor Caius. Stage directions require the opening of a door in seven other plays: *A Woman Is a Weathercock* (III); *The Honest Lawyer* (IV); *The Traitor* (V); *The Duke's Mistress* (V); *Brennoralt* (*The Discontented Colonel*) (V); *The Goblins* (II); *The Guardian* (III); The *Scene* is opened to make a discovery in *A Jovial Crew* [or *The Merry Beggars*] (I, II). Stage directions require that a door be *locked* in five plays: *The Fatal Dowry* (III, V); *The Traitor* (V); *The Goblins* (II); *The Captain* (IV.iv); *The Weeding of the Covent Garden* (IV); A door is *shut* in *Thomas Lord Cromwell* (C4). An actor *speakes through the keyhole* in *The Alchemist* (III.v), and the notation *Edmund at keyhole* appears in *The Puritan* (IV).

In *Henry the Fifth* (1623 Folio) stage directions and dialogue indicate that doorways are localized as the gates of Harfleur. Movable doors are suggested but not specified for this purpose. Act Three, Scene One (according to modern scene and act divisions), opens with *Enter the King, Exeter, Bedford, and Gloucester. Alarum: Scaling Ladders at Harflew.* The King delivers his "Once more unto the breech" oration, and the scene ends with *Alarum, and Chambers goe off.* Scene Three starts with *Enter the King and all his Traine before the Gates;* the King delivers another oration before *Enter Governour* (l. 43), who surrenders and tells the English to "Enter our Gates" (l. 49). The King orders "Open your Gates" (l. 51), and the scene ends with *Flourish, and enter the Towne.* The Quarto (1600) omits Scene One; in Scene Three the comparable stage directions read *Enter the King and his Lords alarum* and *Enter Governour.* The closing stage direction for this scene is omitted in the Quarto.

The concluding scene of *The Winter's Tale* has *Enter Leontes, Polixenes, Florizell, Perdita, Camillo, Paulina; Hermione (like a Statue:) Lords &c.* (V.iii), but Hermione is probably brought into view at Paulina's line, "behold, and say 'tis well" (l. 20). Later in the scene Leontes says, "Do not draw the curtain" (l. 59), and Paulina twice suggests that she "draw the curtain" (ll. 68, 83), but it remains open until Hermione "stirs" (l. 103) and joins the action of the scene, which ends with *exeunt.*

Henry the Eighth has *Exit Lord Chamberlaine, and the King drawes the Curtaine and sits reading pensively* (II.ii.62). Hangings are *drawn* or *parted* in nineteen other plays: *Sir Giles Goosecap* (V); *The Woman Hater* (V.i); *Westward Ho* (IV); *The Merry Devil of Edmonton* (A3v); *A Mad World My Masters* (II); *The White Devil* (*Vittoria Corombona*) (D4v); *The Lover's Melancholy* (II); *The Emperor of the East* (I.ii); *The Fatal Dowry* (II); *Love's Sacrifice* (II, V); *The Platonic Lovers* (II); *The Wits* (I); *The Unnatural Combat* (V.ii); *The City Match* (III.ii, V.vii); *A Tale of a Tub* (V.x); *Brennoralt* (*The Discontented Colonel*) (II, V); *The Unfortunate Lovers* (V); *The Gentleman of Venice* (III); *The Guardian* (III). Curtains *above* are needed in *The Emperor of the East* (I.i) and *The Unnatural Combat* (V.ii); they may be needed in *Henry the Eighth* (V.ii.34–35).

Falstaffe stands behind the aras in *The Merry Wives of Windsor* (III.iii.93). Actors hide behind an arras or hangings in fifteen other plays: 1 *If You Know Not Me You Know Nobody* (F3); *Volpone* III.vii, V.iii); *Philaster* (II.ii); *The Grateful Servant* (III); *The English Traveller* (IV); *The Traitor* (III); *The Wits* (II); *The Example* (I); *The Duke's Mistress* (V); *The Maid's Revenge* (III); *The Opportunity* (V); *The Noble Stranger* (III); *The Unfortunate Lovers* (IV); *The Noble Gentleman* (III); *The Cardinal* (V).

Although no use is made of the hangings in *The Lady of Pleasure*, the dialogue describes them as portraying stories, perhaps from the Old Testament. Celestina enters with her steward and berates him about the appearance of the room in which she plans to receive visitors:

Celestina. . . . What hangings have we here?
Steward. They are Arras Madam.
Celestina. Impudence I know't
I will have fresher and more rich, not wrought
With faces that may scandalize a Christian
With Jewish stories stufft with Corne and Camells. (I)

A similar allusion is made in *The Knight of the Burning Pestle*, where the following exchange occurs between the Citizen and his Wife:

Wife. . . . now sweet lambe, what
story is that painted upon the cloth? the confutation of Saint Paul?

Citizen. No lambe, that's *Raph* and *Lucrece.*

Wife. Raph and *Lucrece?* which *Raph?* our *Raph?* (E4)

DISCOVERIES

Actors, large properties, or both are discovered in seventeen plays, but neither doors nor hangings are specified for this purpose. *Pericles* has *Cleon shewes Pericles the tombe* (IV.iv.22). Other properties described as *discovered* are a *Bed* in *The Rape of Lucrece* (Gv), *All's Lost by Lust* (IV), *The Traitor* (V), *Monsieur Thomas (Father's Own Son)* (V.iv); a *Cage* in *The Bird in a Cage* (IV); a *Chair* in *The Broken* Heart (III); a *Table* in *Humour out of Breath* (III), *The Insatiate Countess* (I); a *State* in *King John and Matilda* (II); a *Body* in *The Revenger's Tragedy* (I); a *Corpse* in *The White Devil (Vittoria Corombona)* (L). In *How a Man May Choose a Good Wife from a Bad* is found *Mistresse Arthur in the Tombe* (H2), a *Tomb* is also required in *Law Tricks* (V), *Love's Sacrifice* (V), *and The Turk* (I.iii). *The Imposture* has *Nunns Discovered singing* (II); and *The Pilgrim* (V.vi) has *An alter prepar'd.*

The discovery space is localized temporarily for a scene or two in each of twenty-six plays, but these localizations do not continue throughout the play. *Troilus and Cressida* has *Achilles and Patroclus stand in their tent* (III.iii.38); in *The Merry Wives of Windsor*, Simple *steps into the Counting-house* (I.iv.39). This space is localized as a *shop* in eight plays. Of these, three plays use the phrase *enter in a shop* or a similar wording: *The Shoemakers' Holiday* (Gv, F3), *The Honest Whore (The Converted Courtesan)* (B4, E2, E3v, G3v), *The Fleer* (IV), *a shop discovered* appears in three plays: *Greene's Tu Quoque* (I), *A Chaste Maid in Cheapside* (I), *A Mad Couple Well Matched* (III); and in two plays directions read *a shop is opened: 2 If You Know Not Me You Know Nobody* (*2 Queen Elizabeth's Troubles*) (D3), *Match Me in London* (II).

The space is localized as a *study* or *closet* in seventeen plays. Of these, ten plays use the phrase *enter in a study* or a similar wording: *Thomas Lord Cromwell* (Bv, D, E4v); *Satiromastix* (B4); *A Woman Killed with Kindness* (B4); *The Dumb Knight* (III); *Ram Alley* (B3v); *The Two Merry Milkmaids* (I, III); *The Staple of News* (V); *'Tis Pity She's a Whore* (III); *The Maid's Revenge* (III); *The Novella* (I.ii). A *study is discovered* in *Law Tricks* (IV). An actor is *put up* in the study in *Epicene* (*The Silent Woman*) (IV.v), and an actor *is seene sitting at his Table* in *The Staple of News* (V.iv). *More Dissemblers besides Women* (I) has the direction *Enter in a closet,* and in *The Northern Lass* (II.iv) an actor enters *out of the closet. The Goblins* has *Locks him into her closet* (II); later in the same scene *Osabrin bounces thrice at the doore, it flies open. The Devil's Law Case* has *Lockes him into a Closet* (V).

ENTRANCES

Henry the Fifth has *Enter at one doore, King Henry, Exeter, Bedford, Warwicke, and other Lords. At another, Queen Isabel, the King, the Duke of Bourgongne, and other French* (V.ii). *Pericles* has *Enter Pericles at one doore, with all his trayne, Cleon and Dioniza at the other* (IV.iv.22); and *Henry the Eighth* has *Enter the Duke of Norfolke at one doore. At the other, the Duke of Buckingham, and the Lord Aburgavenny* (I.i). A similar wording is found in twenty-four other plays: *Satiromastix* (F4v); 1 *The Honest Whore* (*The Converted Courtesan* (A2, A4); 1 *If You Know Not Me You Know Nobody* (E3v); 2 *If You Know Not Me You Know Nobody* (2 *Queen Elizabeth's Troubles* (H, K); *The Puritan* (I); *The Fleer* (III, IV, V); *The Rape of Lucrece* (H2); *A Mad World My Masters* (II); *The Dumb Knight* (I, V); *The Turk* (I); *The White Devil* (*Vittoria Corombona*) (H2, K4v); *The Insatiate Countess* (I); *The Devil's Law Case* (V); *A Chaste Maid in Cheapside* (V); *All's Lost by Lust* (V); *Love's Sacrifice* (III); *The English Traveller* (III, IV); *Monsieur Thomas* (*Father's Own Son*) (I.i); *The Noble Stranger* (III); *The Captain* (III.v); *The Imposture* (I); *The Cardinal* (I); *King John and Matilda* (III); *The Guardian* (V).

Henry the Eighth has *Enter two Gentlemen at severall Doores* (II.i). A similar wording is found in seventeen other plays: 1 *The Honest Whore* (*The Converted Courtesan*) (I3); *Law Tricks* (III); *The Turk* (II.iii); *The Insatiate Countess* (I, II, III); *The Honest Lawyer* (III); *Philaster* (I); *A Chaste Maid in Cheapside* (I); *Love's Sacrifice* (V); *The Platonic Lovers* (II, V); *Monsieur Thomas* (*Father's Own Son*) (V.vi); *The Unnatural Combat* (III.i, II.ii); *The City Match* (II); *The Unfortunate Lovers* (IV); *The Goblins* (I); *The Noble Gentleman* (IV); *The Imposture* (I); *The Cardinal* (IV).

Pass over the stage or a similar wording is found in twenty-five plays:

The Shoemakers' Holiday (C); *Thomas Lord Cromwell* (E3v); 1 *If You Know Not Me You Know Nobody* (G3v); *The Puritan* (I); *A Woman Killed with Kindness* (C2v); *The Rape of Lucrece* (E2v); *The Dumb Knight* (II); *Epicene (The Silent Woman)* (III.vii); *The White Devil (Vittoria Corombona)* (E2, H4); *Greene's Tu Quoque* (I); *The Two Merry Milkmaids* (V); *The Lover's Melancholy* (I); *Match Me in London* (II); *The Fatal Dowry* (II); *Love's Sacrifice* (III); *The Broken Heart* (I, III); *Monsieur Thomas (Father's Own Son)* (II.ii); *Brennoralt (The Discontented Colonel)* (II); *The Goblins* (IV); *The Noble Gentleman* (IV); *A Jovial Crew* [or *The Merry Beggars*] (IV); *A Mad Couple Well Matched* (IV.iv); *The Novella* (II.ii); *The Imposture* (I); *The Cardinal* (IV).

LARGE PROPERTIES

Henry the Eighth has *Hoboies. A small Table under a State for the Cardinall, a longer Table for the Guests. Then Enter Anne Bullen, and divers other Ladies & Gentlemen, as Guests at one Doore; at another Doore enter Sir Henry Guilford* (I.iv); and later in the play *A Councell Table brought in with Chayres and Stooles, and placed under the State. Enter Lord Chancellour, places himselfe at the upper end of the Table, on the left hand: A Seate being left void above him, as for Canterburies Seate. Duke of Suffolke, Duke of Norfolke, Surrey, Lord Chamberlaine, Gardiner, seat themselves in Order on each side. Cromwell at lower end, as Secretary* (V.iii).

Banquets, Tables, and Chairs. These are *brought on* or *set forth* in twenty-two other plays: *Thomas Lord Cromwell* (D2); *Satiromastix* (G4, K3v, K4v); 1 *The Honest Whore (The Converted Courtesan)* (F4v); 2 *If You Know Not Me You Know Nobody (2 Queen Elizabeth's Troubles)* (E4v); *The Revenger's Tragedy* (IV); *A Woman Killed with Kindness* (F); *A Woman Is a Weathercock* (III, V); *The Devil's Law Case* (III); *The Grateful Servant* (IV, V); *The Emperor of the East* (IV.iii); *The Broken Heart* (IV.iv); *The English Traveller* (IV); *'Tis Pity She's a Whore* (IV, V); *The Platonic Lovers* (II, IV); *The Unnatural Combat* (II.ii); *The Noble Stranger* (IV); *The Goblins* (III); *The Captain* (IV.iv); *The Imposture* (V); *The Cardinal* (V); *The Gentleman of Venice* (IV); *King John and Matilda* (III).

Bar. One is needed in *The Two Merry Milkmaids* (III.ii).

Bed. One is *thrust out* in *The Two Merry Milkmaids* (IV.iii) and *A Chaste Maid in Cheapside* (III); it is *put forth* in *A Mad Couple Well Matched* (IV.iii). In *The Wits* (III) a *Couch* is *carried in.* A *bed* or *couch* is needed in nine other plays, but the texts do not specify how it is introduced: 1 *If You Know Not Me You Know Nobody* (B2); *A Woman Killed with Kindness* (H2v); *Volpone* (III); *A Mad World My Masters* (III); *The Dumb Knight* (III); *The White Devil* (*Vittoria Corombona*) (G4v, Kv); *The Devil's Law Case* (III); *'Tis Pity She's a Whore* (V); *The Maid's Revenge* (V).

Body, Coffin, Funeral, or Hearse. One is needed in eleven plays: *The Puritan* (IV); *Law Tricks* (IV, V); *The Turk* (I.iii); *The Insatiate Countess* (V); *A Chaste Maid in Cheapside* (V); *The Devil's Law Case* (V); *The Fatal Dowry* (II); *All's Lost by Lust* (V); *The Bird in a Cage* (V); *The Cardinal* (III); *King John and Matilda* (V).

Others. *The Merry Wives of Windsor* has *Enter Mistresse Ford, with two of her men, and a great buckbasket* (III.iii), and later in the scene *Sir John goes into the basket, they put cloathes over him, the two men carry it away* (l.150). Later in the play *Enter M. Ford, Page, Priest, Shallow, the two men carries the basket, and Ford meets it* (IV.ii.109). *Pericles* has *Enter two or three with a Chest* (III.ii.48). They open it to find Thaisa within, and when *Shee moves* (l. 104), *They carry her away. Exeunt omnes* (l. 112). A chest is needed for similar business in *The Wits* (IV, V). *Henry the Eighth* needs a *State* and a *Canopy,* which is also needed in *Satiromastix* (K4), 1 *If You Know Not Me You Know Nobody* (G3), and *A Woman Is a Weathercock* (III). Other properties needed are an *Altar* in *Match Me in London* (II) and *The Pilgrim* (V.vi); *Armor hung from Trees* in *The Gentleman of Venice* (V); a *Bush* in *The Honest Lawyer* (V); and *Philaster* (IV); a *Bower* in *The Faithful Shepherdess* (V); a *Carpet* in *A Woman Killed with Kindness* (D4v); a *Carpet* and *Cusions* in *The White Devil* (*Vittoria Corombona*) (B4v); a *Hamper* in *King John and Matilda* (II); a Scaffold in *The Dumb Knight* (III) and *The Insatiate Countess* (V); a *Tree* in *The Honest Lawyer* (V) and *The Cardinal* (V); a *Vaulting Horse* in *The White Devil* (*Vittoria Corombona*) (D4v).

ABOVE THE STAGE

In *Henry the Eighth* is found *Enter the King, and Buts, at a Windowe above* (V.ii.16). This acting space is referred to as *above* or *aloft* in twenty-seven other plays: 1 *If You Know Not Me You Know Nobody* (Gv); *The Woman Hater* (IV.iii); *The Puritan* (V); *Westward Ho* (IV); *Volpone* (II.ii); *Humour out of Breath* (V); *The Dumb Knight* (I, IV); *The Turk* (I, IV); *A Woman Is a Weathercock* (III); *Epicene* (*The Silent Woman*) (IV.ii); *Greene's Tu Quoque* (C4v, F, Fv); *Philaster* (II); *Love's Sacrifice* (II, V), *'Tis Pity She's a Whore* (I, III, V); *The Traitor* (IV); *The Example* (III); *Monsieur Thomas* (*Father's Own Son*) (III.iii); *The Unnatural Combat* (II.i); *The Maid's Revenge* (III, IV); *The Opportunity* (II); *The Noble Stranger* (II); *The Goblins* (V); *The Captain* (IV.iv, V.ii); *The Novella* (II.ii, V.i); *King John and Matilda* (I, V); *More Dissemblers besides Women* (I.iii); *The Weeding of the Covent Garden* (II.ii). It is referred to as a *window* in four plays: *The Insatiate Countess* (III); *A Tale of a Tub* (I.i); *The Captain* (II.ii); *The Novella* (IV.i). It is referred to as a *tarras* in *The White Devil* (*Vittoria Corombona*) (H2), as a *Bellconie* in *The Weeding of Covent Garden* (I), and as *the walls* in *Humour out of Breath* (V) and *King John and Matilda* (V). Directions for *music above* are found in *The Northern Lass* (II.iii); *The Fatal Dowry* (IV); *The Opportunity* (II). Actors *descend* from *above* in four plays: *The Dumb Knight* (I); *Epicene* (*the Silent Woman*) (IV.ii); *The Turk* (IV); *The Unnatural Combat* (II.i). The term *upper stage* occurs in only one play probably first performed by professionals in the years 1599–1642: in *Humour out of Breath* is found *Enter Aspero like Hortensio, Florimell, and Assistance on the upper stage* (IV).

5 Below the Stage

Access to the space *below* the stage is required in forty-two plays, some of which also require an acting area *above*, or a discovery space, or both. In some plays this opening is described fictionally as a *well*, a *gulf*, a *ditch*, a *pit*, a *vault*, or a *grave*; in other plays it is described theatrically as *below* or *under the stage*. A rectangular marking on the floor of the stage in the *Messalina* drawing suggests the outline of a trap door. The *Roxana*, *Wits*, Swan, Cockpit-in-Court and Jones/Webb drawings all show a platform stage that can be fitted with a trap door to the place *below*.

At Trinity Hall, the area under the gallery has a clearance of only six feet, five inches. For this reason Prouty states: "No platform or scaffolding could have been erected, and there would be little need of any, because we may assume that the spectators were seated on the benches which were part of the furniture of the Hall. Even though the players might use part of the floor in front of the gallery, there would remain ample room for an audience of two hundred."[1] Though it is true that the sight lines for a seated audience would probably be adequate without a platform stage, it would be necessary to improvise staging procedures for plays that require access to the place below. For example, in *Hamlet* the staging of *Ghost cries under the stage* (I.v.148) might—with minor line changes—be performed with the Ghost speaking from *within*. The Graveyard Scene (V.i) would require more drastic textual changes, however.

79

Promptbooks, manuscripts dependent on prompt copy, and printed texts with manuscript prompter's markings, for plays first acted by professionals in the years 1599–1642. Listed in presumed order of first performance.

Macbeth (404), Shakespeare, (collection) 1623 (Padua). King's men at the Globe, 20 April 1611 (Chambers, *WS*, II, 337–338). "That behind F there lies a prompt-book of some sort is . . . beyond reasonable doubt." Greg, *Folio*, p. 395. Prompter's markings have been added to the Padua copy of Folio; see G. Blakemore Evans, "New Evidence on the Provenance of the Padua Prompt-Books of Shakespeare's *Macbeth, Measure for Measure,* and *Winter's Tale,*" *SB*, 20:239–242(1967). I cite the collotype facsimile in *Shakespearean Prompt-Books of the Seventeenth Century*, I, ed. G. Blakemore Evans, (Charlottesville: Bibliographical Society of the University of Virginia, 1960).

The Two Noble Ladies (MS), Anonymous (British Museum). Revels company at the Red Bull, 1619–1623 (Bentley, V, 1426–1427). I cite the edition of R. G. Rhoads, who states: "The actual use of the manuscript in the playhouse is proved by a number of marginal annotations by the prompter or stage manager. . . The chief interest of these notes is that they preserve the names of five actors who took part in some performance of the piece. . . The prompter has on several occasions repeated in the left margin directions which the author had written on the right." MSR (London, 1930), pp. vii–ix. See also Greg, *Documents*, I, 229–231.

Believe As You List (MS), Massinger (British Museum). Refused Revels license by Herbert, 11 January 1630/1; MS. carries Revels license, 6 May 1631; King's men, 7 May 1631 (Bentley, IV, 762–765). I cite the edition of C. J. Sisson, who states: "It bears the autograph license of the Master of the Revels, it is corrected and prepared for acting by a stage-adapter, and shows all the processes through which the copy passed on its way from the author to the prompter. It is an invaluable document to the historian of the stage as well as of the drama." MSR (London, 1927), p. v. See also Greg, *Documents*, I, 293–300.

The Lost Lady (MS), Berkeley (Folger). At Court and Blackfriars, before 7 February 1637/8; King's men at the Cockpit-in-Court, 26 March 1638 (Bentley, III, 23–25). "Both texts [MS and F] were derived from the theatrical prompt-copy, and . . . originally the scribe of the manuscript for presentation to the Queen, like the compositor of the folio, incorporated into his version the prompter's directions he found in his copy." R. C. Bald, "Sir William Berkeley's *The Lost Lady*," *Library*, 4th ser. 17:407(1937).

Plays first acted by professionals in the years 1599– 1642 and first printed during 1600–1659 from prompt copy or texts that may depend wholly or in part on prompt copy. Listed in order of first printing.

Hamlet (197), Shakespeare, (collection) 1623 (Columbia). Revels Office records, ca. 1619–20. King's men at Hampton Court, 24 January 1636/7 (Chambers, *WS*, II, 346, 353). TP (Q1, 1603): "As it hath beene diverse times acted by his Highnesse servants in the Cittie of London: as also in the two Universities of Cambridge and Oxford and else-where"; (Q2, 1604–5):"Newly imprinted and enlarged to almost as much againe as it was, according to the true and perfect Coppie." Greg summarizes conjectures about the probable source of printer's copy for the various texts as follows: "There is now very general agreement that Q1 is a reported text and represents a version of the play acted by a company touring in the country . . . The theory that it was Shakespeare's original manuscript that was handed to the printer has perhaps been more widely accepted in the case of the second quarto of *Hamlet* than in that of any other edition of a play of the canon, and seeing that the print can hardly have been in any way derived from the prompt-book, it can claim a high degree of inherent probability. . . If Q2 was printed from Shakespeare's foul papers and F was not printed from Q2, it would seem likely that F was printed from, or at least had behind it, the official prompt-book, and this view has indeed been widely accepted, though the evidence in its favour is not altogether clear. . . On the whole it seems to be a rather queer prompt-book, if prompt-book it is, that lies behind F. The editing is at times competent and even adroit, at times bungled and ineffective. . . Wilson's theory that F was printed not from the prompt-book itself but from a copy of it made for the purpose, is plausible enough if the company, as it is only reasonable to assume, was unwilling to part with the original. . . This problem is taken up by Alice Walker in her recent discussion of the play. She accepts the substance of Wilson's findings, including the transcript of the original prompt-copy; on the other hand, she believes this transcript to have been made for the theatre to replace a worn-out prompt-book, and F to have been printed from a copy of Q2 that had been altered and corrected by comparison with it." Greg, *Folio*, pp. 300–328. See also Harold Jenkins, "Playhouse Interpolations in the Folio Text of *Hamlet*," *SB*, 13:31–47(1960). In a more recent study J. M. Nosworthy suggests: "The Folio version must be accepted as theatrical and therefore authoritative, but there is manifest need for emendation." Nosworthy, *Shakespeare's Occasional Plays: Their Origin and Transmission* (New York: Barnes and Noble, 1965), p. 222.

Bussy D'Ambois (246), Chapman, 1641 (Huntington). (Chambers, III, 253–254). TP (Q1, 1607): Paul's boys. "[Q1] is well and tidily printed and reasonably free from obvious misprints. It has several of the characteristics of a text printed from author's manuscript rather than from a theatre prompt-book. . . [Q2, 1641] on the other hand, for all its extensive differences, is not derived direct from a manuscript, but from a corrected copy of [Q1] . . . by reference to a manuscript . . . [that] seems to have been a prompt-book which had been used in the theatre in the 1630's." Nicholas Brooke, ed., *The Revels Plays* (Cambridge: Harvard University Press, 1964), pp. lxi–lxiv.

The Atheist's Tragedy (293), Tourneur, 1611 (Folger). (Chambers, III, 499). TP: "In divers places." "It is difficult to come to any certain conclusions about the provenance of the quarto, but one not impossible hypothesis may be that a fair copy of Tourneur's manuscript, not itself prepared for use in the theatre, was used as a prompt-copy by some provincial company." Irving Ribner, ed., *The Revels Plays* (Cambridge: Harvard University Press, 1964), p. xxvii.

If It Be Not Good the Devil Is in It (305), Dekker with Daborne, 1612 (British Museum). (Chambers, III, 297). TP: Queen Anne's men at the Red Bull. "No precision of assignment is possible, but it might appear that the printer's manuscript was either a worked-over set of autograph papers preceding the preparation of the prompt-book, or else a rather rough autograph manuscript serving itself as the prompt-book." Bowers, *Dekker*, III, 116.

Cymbeline (406), Shakespeare, (collection) 1623 (Columbia). At the Globe?, 1611; at St. James, 1 January 1633/4 (Chambers, *WS*, II, 338–339, 352). "Most critics regard the vision in V.iv. (ll. 30–126?— the later limit is disputed) as what Chambers, who agrees, calls 'a spectacular theatrical interpolation.' If this is so, and if the interpolation is of later date, the manuscript containing it can hardly have been Shakespeare's foul papers, and we must see behind F the company's prompt-book as it stood in the early twenties. This is in accord with the rest of the evidence. The actual copy may, of course, have been an *ad hoc* transcript." Greg, *Folio*, pp. 413–414. Dr. Alice Walker finds "certain features of the Folio text difficult to reconcile with the prompt-book theory." Her unpublished comments are cited by J. M. Nosworthy, ed., *The Arden Shakespeare* (Cambridge: Harvard University Press, 1955), p. xii.

The Two Noble Kinsmen (492), Fletcher and Shakespeare, 1634 (Huntington). Revels Office records, ca. 1619–20 (Chambers, *WS*, II, 346). TP: King's men at Blackfriars. "A quarto evidently printed from a prompt-copy written or at least annotated by Edward Knight, bookkeeper in the King's company." Greg, *Folio*, p. 98. "Whereas the printed text does show unmistakable signs of the prompter's hand in marginal warning notes and in actors' names, it also exhibits certain other textual peculiarities that point to foul papers." Frederick O. Waller, "Printer's Copy for *The Two Noble Kinsmen*," *SB*, 11:61 (1958). Paul Bertram rejects Waller's hypothesis and states: "No doubt anything is 'possible,' but the assumption of a single manuscript in Shakespeare's hand which served as the prompt-book on more than one occasion provides a thoroughly satisfactory and unified explanation of all the bibliographical data, and there is no need to multiply extravagant *ad hoc* hypotheses." *Shakespeare and The Two Noble Kinsmen* (New Brunswick, N. J.: Rutgers University Press, 1965), p. 121.

The Prophetess (654), Fletcher with Massinger?, (collection) 1647

(Columbia). Revels license, 14 May 1622; King's men, 21 July 1629; protected for King's men, 7 August 1641 (Bentley, III, 394–397). "Evidence is . . . sufficient to justify . . . conjectural inclusion among the prompt-copies." Bald, *Folio*, p. 108.

Bonduca (655), Fletcher, (collection) 1647 (Columbia). Protected for King's men, 7 August 1641 (Bentley, I, 109); "The actor list is of the King's men between 1609–11 or between 1613–14" (Chambers, III, 228). "At first glance there is nothing in the folio stage directions to suggest performance, but a comparison of them with those of the manuscript soon shows that the whole play has been thoroughly gone over by a producer. . . In view of all these additions in the folio one can safely assert that careful attention to musical effects and noises off stage in a text is an indication that it has received the producer's attention, and is probably derived from a prompt-copy." Bald, *Folio*, 78–79.

BELOW THE STAGE

A prompter's warning in *Believe As You List* reads: "Gascoine: & Hubert below: ready to open the Trap doore for Mr. Taylor" (p. 60). Twelve speeches later is another prompter's warning: "Antiochus— ready: under the stage" (p. 62). In the next scene a jailer enters and calls to Antiochus, who answers from "belowe." The dialogue suggests that Antiochus rises from his dungeon to play the rest of the scene on stage. *The Lost Lady* has "The Ghost ariseth" (IV). In *The Prophetess* Delphia says, "Mount up my birds; some rites I am to perform to Hecate," followed by the marginal direction *Ascend* (II.iii); later in the play, *Enter a Spirit from the Well* (V.iii). The space below is fitted out with fire effects in *The Two Noble Ladies*. Justina is beset by fiends, but an angel enters and "The Devills sinck roaring; a flame of fier riseth after them" (p. 73). Shortly after this, Cyprian, a magician, rejects his art; the stage direction reads "Throws his charmed rod, and his booke under the stage, a flame riseth" (p. 74). *Bonduca* has *A flame arises* (III).

A trap to the place below was probably used for staging scenes in which actors *vanish*. *Macbeth* has *Witches vanish* followed by Banquo's line "The Earth hath bubbles, as the Water ha's" (I.iii.78), which strongly implies that the actors drop through a trap. This would also be useful for Banquo's Ghost who appears and disappears in the Banquet Scene (III.iv),[2] for the Apparitions who speak and then *descend* (IV.i.72, 80, 93), and for *The Witches Dance and vanish* (IV.i.132). *Hamlet* (F) has *Ghost cries under the Stage* (I.v.148), and after the burial of Ophelia, Laertes *Leaps in the grave* (V.i.273). *The Atheist's Tragedy* has *D'amville thrusts him downe into the gravell pit* (II) and *Borachio descends* and *ascends* [from "underneath the bank"] (II). *The Two Noble Kinsmen* has *Here the Hynde vanishes under the Altar; and in the place ascends a Rose Tree, having one Rose upon it. . . Here is heard a sodaine twang of Instruments, and the Rose falls from the Tree* (V.i.163,168). Whereupon, Emilia says, "The flowre is falne, the Tree descends." In *Cymbeline*, Ghosts *circle Posthumus as he lies sleeping* and as the vision ends they *Vanish* (V.iv.122). *Bussy D'Ambois* has *Ascendit Frier and D'Ambois* and *Descendit Fryar* (II); *Ascendit Frier* and *Descendit Frier* (III). After a Latin incantation by the Friar, Behemoth *Ascendit* and, later, *Descendit cum suis* (IV); still later Montsurry *puts the Frier in the vault and follows* (V). Only one text that may depend on playhouse copy requires more than one trap. *If It Be Not Good the Devil Is in It* has *The play* [within the play] *ending, as they goe off, from under the ground in severall places, rise up spirits, to them enter, leaping in great joy, Rufman, Shaklesoule, and Lurchall, discovering behind a curten, Ravillac, Guy Faulx, Bartervile a Prodigall, standing in their torments* (L3). The traps are used several times earlier in this play: *Ruffman comes up, Furie enters* (B2); *Enter Shackle-soule comes up* (B2); *Lurchall and another Spirit comes up* (B2); *Golden head ascends* (C3, F3v); *Descendit* (F3v); *Golden head ascends* (G3); *Sinck downe, above flames* (L2v).

At one door and . . . at the other or a similar wording is found in five plays. *The Two Noble Ladies* has "Enter at one Dore the Souldan with souldiers, from the other a Herald meets him, delivers him a paper" (p. 61); "Enter at one dore the Souldan, Colactus, & Souldiers at the other the Califfe, a Nobleman, Herald, & Souldier" (p. 75); "Enter Claudius with Souldiers at one dore, surpriseth the Califfe; Clitophon with souldiers, at the other, he seazeth the Souldan, enter Cyprian and

Justina" (p. 80); also "Exeunt severally" (p. 42) and "The Souldan and Herald goe of severally" (p. 80). In *Cymbeline* there are *Enter in State, Cymbeline, Queene, Clotten, and Lords at one doore, and at another, Caius, Lucius, and Attendants* (III.i); *Enter Lucius, Iachimo, and the Romane Army at one doore: and the Britaine Army at another: Leonatus Posthumus following like a poore Souldier. They march over, and goe out. Then enter againe in Skirmish Iachimo and Posthumus: he vanquisheth and disarmeth Iachimo, and then leaves him* (V.ii). *Bussy D'Ambois* has *Exeunt severally* (V). In *The Prophetess* actors appear in a dumb show *at one door* and *at the other door* (IV). *The Atheist's Tragedy* has *Music. A banquet. In the night. Enter D'amville, Belforest, Levidulcia, Rousard, Castabella, Languebeau Snuffe, at one doore; at the other doore, Cataplasma and Soquette, usher'd by Fresco* (II).

Pass over the stage or a similar wording is found in two plays. *Macbeth* has *Enter a Sewer, and divers Servants with Dishes and Service over the Stage. Then enter Macbeth* (I.vii). *Cymbeline* has *They march over, and goe out* (V.ii). *The Atheist's Tragedy* has *Enter Borachio warily and hastily over the Stage, with a stone in eyther hand* (II).

LARGE PROPERTIES

Banquets, Tables, Chairs, and Stools. These are *brought on* or *set forth* in six plays. *Macbeth* has *Banquet prepar'd. Enter Macbeth, Lady, Rosse, Lenox, Lords, and Attendants* (III.iv); *Hamlet* has *Enter King, Queene, Laertes and Lords, with other Attendants with Foyles, and Gauntlets, a Table and Flagons of Wine on it* (V.ii.235). *Believe As You List* has a prompter's warning "Table ready: & 6 chaires to sett out" (p. 23), which anticipates the council scene following (p. 25); later comes "chaires set out" (p. 59). *The Two Noble Kinsmen* has *Enter Theseus, Hipolita, Emilia, Arcite, in a chaire* (V.iv.85); *Bussy D'Ambois* has *Montsurry bare, unbrac't pulling Tamyra in by the haire, Frier, One bearing light, a standish and paper, which sets a Table* (V.i). A banquet is needed in *The Atheist's Tragedy* (II).

Bed. *The Lost Lady* has the notation "The Bed thrust out" in the margin next to the stage direction "Enter the Moore on her bed Hermione Phillida & Irene & Servants about her" (V). *Cymbeline* has *Enter*

Imogen, in her Bed, and a Lady (II.ii). *The Atheist's Tragedy* has *A bed drawne forth with Rousard* (V).

Body, Coffin, or Hearse. *Hamlet* has *Enter King, Queene, Laertes, and a Coffin, with Lords attendant* (V.i.241); *The Two Noble Kinsmen* has the notation on C3v *2 Hearses ready with Palamon: and Arcite: the 3 Queenes. Theseus and his Lordes ready,* which anticipates the direction on C4v. *Enter the Queenes with the Hearses of their Knightes, in a Funerall Solempnity &c.* *The Atheist's Tragedy* has *Enter with the murdered body* (II), *Enter the Funerall of Montferrers* (III), *Enter the Funerall of Charlemont as a soldier* (III), *Enter Servants with the body of Sebastian* (V), and *Enter D'amville distractedly, with the hearses of his two Sonnes borne after him* (V).

Others. *Macbeth* has *Enter Malcolme, Seyward, Macduffe, and their Army, with Boughes* (V.vi). In *Hamlet* the dumb show requires a *Banke of Flowers* on which the Player King can lie (III.ii.145). *Cymbeline* has *Iachimo from the Trunke* (II.ii). In *The Two Noble Kinsmen* Palomon *Lies on the Blocke* (V.iv.38). *The Prophetess* needs a *Litter* (II.iii) and a *Throne drawn by Dragons* (II.iii). A *Tree* is needed in *If It Be Not Good the Devil Is in It* (I). *The Atheist's Tragedy* needs a *Scaffold* (V).

ABOVE THE STAGE

In *Believe As You List* the prompter's warning "Enter: Metellus— fflaminius: & Sempronius (Above)" is followed after twenty lines by "Enter above flaminius metellus sempronius" (p. 65), *The Lost Lady* has "whilst he kneeles Hermione and the Moore looke downe from the windowe" (III). *Bussy D'Ambois* has *Enter Monsieur and Guise above* (V). *The Two Noble Kinsmen* has *Enter Palomon, and Arcite above* (II.i). In *The Wonder of Women* occurs *Musique above* (IV). *The Prophetess* has *A hand with a Bolt appears above* and later in the scene *The hand taken in* (V.iii). *Bonduca* has *Daughters above* (II.iii) and *Bonduca, two daughters and Neunius, above* (III.iv). *Cymbeline* has *Jupiter descends in Thunder and Lightning, sitting uppon an Eagle; hee throwes a Thunder-bolt. The Ghostes fall on their knees* (V.iv.92); after his speech of twenty-one lines Jupiter *Ascends.*

DOORS OR HANGINGS

The prompter's anticipatory directions in *Believe As You List* read "Harry: Willson: & Boy ready for the song at ye Arras" (p. 65). Later in the scene there is the prompter's notation "the Lute, strikes & then the Songe," followed by the direction "Ent: Courtezan" (p. 67). Apparently the song is used as a cue for her entrance, but the singer and the lute-player remain hidden behind the arras. *Bussy D'Ambois* has a prompter's anticipatory marking *Table Chesbord & Tapers behind the Arras* (I.i). The stage directions in Folio *Hamlet* do not specify the use of the arras for the scene in which Hamlet kills Polonius, but in the preceding scene Polonius says to the King:

> My Lord, he's going to his Mothers Closset:
> Behinde the Arras Ile convey my selfe
> To heare the Processe."   (III.iii.27–29)

In *Bussy D'Ambois* Tamyra *raps her self in the Arras* (V). A curtain is also required for a discovery in *If It Be Not Good the Devil Is in It* (L3). *The Atheist's Tragedy* has *Fresco hides himselfe* and *Fresco peepes fearfully forth from behinde the Arras* (II).

In an early scene in *The Two Noble Ladies* comes the direction "Alarm still Crie within, Kill Kill Kill Enter Barebones (a poore Scholler) running." More shouts of "Kill" are heard, and Barebones says, "Ile runne into my masters study, and hide mee in his inckhorne" (p. 6). Here the prompter notes "Ciprian discovered at his booke." Barebones pleads for shelter and Ciprian "hides him under the table" (p. 7). Apparently the scene ends here, because Lysander and Miranda enter and play an unlocalized scene not related to Barebone's escape. In another unlocalized scene later in the play, Ciprian says to Cantharides, "Let me see this Christian Saint which I am forc'd to worship." The stage direction reads "Justina is discovered in a chaire asleep, in her hands a prayer booke, divvels about her" (p. 69). She awakens and the devils continue a pantomime until an angel appears and they "sinck roaring." *The Lost Lady* has "The Tombe discovered" (I). *Bonduca* has *Enter Caratach upon a rock, and Hengo by him, sleeping* (V.i); *Enter Caratach and Hengo on the Rock,* and *Enter Petillius & Junius on the rock* (V.iii). *The Atheist's Tragedy* has *Enter Castabella mourning to the monument of Charlemont* (III) and *Charlemont findes his Fathers Monument* (III), Charlemont *Hides himselfe in the Charnell house* (IV), and *A Clozet discover'd. A servant sleeping with lights and money before him* (V).

Other plays first acted by professionals in the years 1599–1642 and first printed during 1600–1659. Listed in order of first printing.

Antonio's Revenge (185), Marston, 1602 (Pforzheimer). (Chambers, III, 429–430). TP: Paul's boys.

Poetaster (186), Jonson, (collection) 1616 (Huntington). (Chambers, III, 364–366). TP (1616): Chapel Children in 1601.

A Larum for London (192), Anonymous, 1602 (Huntington). (Chambers, IV, 1). TP: Chamberlain's men.

The Wonder of Women (*Sophonisba*) (231), Marston, 1606 (Huntington). (Chambers, III, 433). TP: Blackfriars.

The Whore of Babylon (241), Dekker, 1607 (Huntington). (Chambers, III, 296). TP: Prince Henry's men. "There can be little doubt that the printer's copy was Dekker's own manuscript." Bowers, *Dekker*, II, 493.

The Devil's Charter (254), Barnes, 1607 (Huntington). (Chambers, III, 214–215). TP: "As it was plaide before the Kings Maiestie, upon Candlemassse night last: by his Majesties Servants. But more exactly renewed, corrected and augmented since by the Author, for the more pleasure and profit of the Reader."

The Faithful Shepherdess (287), Fletcher, 1610? (Huntington). King's men at Court, 6 January 1633/4 (Chambers, III, 221–222). TP (1634). At Somerset House and Blackfriars.

Catiline His Conspiracy (296), Jonson, (collection) 1616 (Huntington).

At Court, 9 November 1634 (Bentley, I, 121, Chambers, III, 372). TP (Q2, 1635) : King's men.

The Revenge of Bussy D'Ambois (307), Chapman, 1613 (Huntington). (Chambers, III, 258). TP: Whitefriars.

The Knight of the Burning Pestle (316), Beaumont, 1613 (British Museum). Queen Henrietta's men at St. James, 28 February 1635/6 (Adams, *Herbert,* p. 56; Chambers, III, 220–221). TP (Q2, 1635) : Queen Henrietta's men at the Phoenix. "There is evidence to suggest that [Q] had as its copy the author's manuscript." John Doebler, ed. (Lincoln: University of Nebraska Press, 1967), p. xxiii.

The Valiant Welshman (327), Anonymous, 1615 (Huntington). (Chambers, IV, 51). TP: Prince Charles's (II) men.

The Maid's Tragedy (357), Beaumont and Fletcher, 1619 (Huntington). Revels Office records, ca. 1619–20; King's men at Court, 9 December 1630 and 29 November 1636 (Bentley, I, 113; Chambers, III, 224–225). TP: King's men at Blackfriars. "The ultimate source of this first edition appears to be foul papers." Howard B. Norland, ed. (Lincoln: University of Nebraska Press, 1968), p. xxiv.

The Virgin Martyr (380), Dekker with Massinger, 1622 (Huntington). Revels license for "new reforming," 6 October 1620 (Bentley, III, 263–266). TP: Red Bull (Revels) company. "This manuscript was apparently not a theatrical one. No signs of professional intervention appear, and no one has troubled to remove the redundant character identifications from Dekker's stage direction heading II.ii or the direction following II.iii.56." Bowers, *Dekker,* III, 367.

The Duchess of Malfy (389), Webster, 1623 (British Museum). (Chambers, III, 510–511). TP: King's men at Blackfriars and the Globe. "The perfect and exact coppy, with diverse things Printed, that the length of the Play would not beare in the Presentment." "We may conclude that the copy for *The Duchess of Malfi* was a transcript, probably in the hand of Ralph Crane, and that the text had been so prepared that no clear sign of foul papers or prompt-book has survived. It is also probable that the author was responsible for the publication, which was undertaken with the consent of the players." J. R. Brown, "The Printing of John Webster's Plays (I)," *SB*, 6:137(1953).

The Tempest (390), Shakespeare, (collection) 1623 (Columbia). King's men at Whitehall, 1 November 1611; King's men at Court, winter of 1612–13, payment, 20 May 1613 (Chambers, *WS*, II, 342–343). "Crane's transcript was clearly made from the author's original. This must have been carefully prepared and might have served as a prompt-copy. But if the book-keeper annotated it to any extent for the stage, Crane edited away all traces of his handiwork." Greg, *Folio*, p. 420.

The Renegado (430), Massinger, 1630 (Huntington). Revels license for the Phoenix, 17 April 1624; protected for Beeston's boys, 10 August 1639 (Bentley, IV, 811–815). TP: Queen Henrietta's men at the Phoenix.

The Duchess of Suffolk (451), Drue, 1631 (Library of Congress). Revels license and censorship, Palsgrave's men, 2 January 1623/4 (Bentley, III, 284–286).

The Devil Is an Ass (457), Jonson, (collection) 1631 (Huntington). (Bentley, IV, 614–617). TP: King's men.

The Martyred Soldier (533), Henry Shirley, 1638 (University of Michigan). (Bentley, V, 1060–1062). TP: The Phoenix and other theaters.

The Seven Champions of Christendom (545), Kirke, 1638 (Huntington). (Bentley, IV, 712–714). TP: The Phoenix and Red Bull.

Arviragus and Philicia (551 & 552), Carlell, 1639 (Huntington). Part Two, King's men for the Queen at Blackfriars, between November 1635 and May 1636; Part Two at Court, 16 February 1635/6; Parts One and Two, King's men at the Cockpit-in-Court, 18 and 19 April 1636; Part One, King's men at Hampton Court, 26 December 1636;

Part Two, King's men at Hampton Court, 27 December 1636 (Bentley, III, 113–115). TP: King's men at Blackfriars.

The Bloody Banquet (567), Drue?, 1639 (Huntington). Protected for Beeston's boys, 10 August 1639 (Bentley, III, 282–284).

Messalina (578), Richards, 1640 (Huntington). (Bentley, V, 1002–1004). TP: King's Revels company.

The Rebellion (582), Rawlins, 1640 (Folger) (Bentley, V, 995–998). TP: Revels company.

The Arcadia (583), James Shirley?, 1640 (Huntington). (Bentley, V, 1073–1076). TP: Queen Henrietta's men at the Phoenix.

Rule a Wife and Have a Wife (598), Fletcher, 1640 (Pforzheimer). Revels license, 19 October 1624; King's men at Court, 2 November 1624; King's men at Whitehall, 26 December 1624; Blackfriars, February 1634/5 (Bentley, III, 407–411). TP: King's men.

The Island Princess (650), Fletcher, (collection) 1647 (Columbia). King's men at Court, 26 December 1621: protected for King's men, 7 August 1641 (Bentley, III, 347–350). "It has not been possible to find any directions which suggest, even remotely, the specific influence of the prompter." Bald, *Folio*, pp. 109–110.

The Humorous Lieutenant (651), Fletcher, (collection) 1647 (Columbia). Protected for King's men, 7 August 1641 (Bentley, III, 343–347). "Two tendencies seem to have been at work to differentiate the stage directions in the two versions of *The Humorous Lieutenant*. Those in the folio are more precise, and every now and then make provision for properties or noises off stage of which the manuscript knows nothing. Crane's directions in the manuscript, on the other hand, seem to have been 'written up' somewhat, with occasional touches of literary elaboration based perhaps on recollections of actual performances of the play; they are, one feels, less curt than the stage directions which a thoroughly experienced dramatist would insert during composition, and they are also written for the reader rather than the actor or producer." Bald, *Folio*, p. 76.

Love and Honour (684), Davenant, 1649 (Folger). Revels license, 20
November 1634; acted 12 December 1634; King's men at Hampton
Court, 1 January 1636/7; protected for King's men, 7 August 1641
(Bentley, III, 205–206). TP: King's men at Blackfriars.

BELOW THE STAGE

The Tempest has *Ariel vanishes in Thunder* (III.iii.82), and figures
of the masque *heavily vanish* (IV.i.138). A space is referred to as *below*
in three plays: *The Devil Is an Ass* (II.vii); *The Bloody Banquet*
(IV.iii); *Rule a Wife and Have a Wife* (V). It is referred to as *under
the stage* in two plays: *Antonio's Revenge* (V.ii); *The Renegado*
(IV.iii). Actors *rise* or *ascend* from the space *below* in ten plays: *Poetas-
ter* (Prologue); *Philotas* (V); *The Wonder of Women* (*Sophonisba*)
(V); *The Devil's Charter* (Prologue and IV.i); *The Faithful Shep-
herdess* (III); *The Knight of the Burning Pestle* (I); *The Maid's
Tragedy* (I); *The Martyred Soldier* (V); *The Bloody Banquet* (IV.iv);
The Humorous Lieutenant (IV.iii). Apparently emerging from a dun-
geon, *King appeares loden with chaines, his head, arms only above* in
The Island Princess (II.i). Actors *descend* or *sink* in eight plays: *The
Wonder of Women* (*Sophonisba*) (III); *The Valiant Welshman*
(II.iv); *The Maid's Tragedy* (I); *The Virgin Martyr* (V); *The Seven
Champions of Christendom* (I); *Messalina* (V); *The Rebellion* (IV);
Love and Honour (III). This space is described fictionally as a *Cave*
in *The Martyred Soldier* (V) and *Love and Honour* (III), as a *Grave*
in *The Duchess of Malfy* (V.iii), as a *gulf* in *The Revenge of Bussy
D'Ambois* (V), as a *pit* in *The Bloody Banquet* (II), as a *well* in
A Larum for London (D4v) and *The Duchess of Suffolk* (III). *Fire
flashes out of the Cave* in *1 Arviragus and Philicia* (V). *A grone of
many people is heard under the ground* in *Catiline His Conspiracy* (I).
An Alter rais'd is found in *2 Arviragus and Philicia* (II); an actor
is *burying the picture* in *The Whore of Babylon* (E3).

ENTRANCES

At one door and . . . at the other or a similar wording appears in
The Wonder of Women (*Sophonisba*) (A3); *The Whore of Babylon*
(F4); *The Devil's Charter* (IV.i); *The Valiant Welshman* (I.iii, II.ii,

II.iv, V.i); *The Renegado* (V.ii); *The Duchess of Suffolk* (I); *1 Arviragus and Philicia* (V); *The Arcadia* (IV); *The Island Princess* (V); *Love and Honour* (V). *Several doors* or *severally* appears in *Antonio's Revenge* (II.ii, V.iii); *The Devil's Charter* (I.i, V.iii); *The Virgin Martyr* (III), *The Duchess of Suffolk* (II); *1 Arviragus and Philicia* (IV); *The Rebellion* (I); *The Island Princess* (II). *Pass over the stage* or a similar wording is found in *Antonio's Revenge* (V.i); *The Revenge of Bussy D'Ambois* (III.i, IV.i); *The Seven Champions of Christendom* (III); *Messalina* (IV).

LARGE PROPERTIES

Banquets, Tables, Chairs, and Stools. In *The Tempest* is found *Solemne and strange Musicke: and Prosper on the top (invisible:)*[3] *Enter severall strange shapes, bringing in a Banket; and dance about it with gentle actions of salutations, and inviting the King, &c. to eate, they depart* (III.iii.16). Later in this scene is found *Thunder and Lightning. Enter Ariell (like a Harpey) claps his wings upon the Table, and with a quient device the Banquet vanishes* (1. 52).[4] After Ariel's long speech as Harpy, *He vanishes in Thunder: then (to soft Musicke.) Enter the shapes againe, and daunce (with mockes and mowes) and carrying out the Table* (1. 82).

These properties are *brought on* or *set forth* in six other plays: *The Devil's Charter* (I.v, IV.iii, V.iv, V.vi); *The Renegado* (II.iv); *The Bloody Banquet* (III.iii, V.vii); *Messalina* (III); *The Rebellion* (IV.v); *Love and Honour* (III).

Bar. One is *set out* in *The Arcadia* (V).

Bed. One is *thrust out* in *The Virgin Martyr* (IV) and *drawn out* in *Messalina* (II). A bed is also needed in six other plays, but the texts do not specify how it is introduced: *The Wonder of Women (Sophonisba)* (I.ii); *The Devil's Charter* (IV.v); *The Valiant Welshman* (V.i); *The Maid's Tragedy* (V); *The Duchess of Malfy* (IV.ii); *The Martyred Soldier* (I, III, V).

Body, Hearse, or Coffin. One is called for in seven plays: *Antonio's Revenge* (II.i); *A Larum for London* (B2); *The Knight of the Burning*

Pestle (IV, V); *The Valiant Welshman* (IV.ii); *The Duchess of Malfy* (IV.ii, V.v); *The Duchess of Suffolk* (IV); *The Seven Champions of Christendom* (III).

Others. An *Altar* appears in *2 Arviragus and Philicia* (II); *Boughs* in *The Island Princess* (II); a *Bush* in *The Duchess of Suffolk* (III); a *Canopy* in *The Whore of Babylon* (A4), *The Seven Champions of Christendom* (III); a *Ladder* in *The Duchess of Suffolk* (II, IV); a *Pillar* in *The Virgin Martyr* (IV); a *Rack* in *The Virgin Martyr* (V), *Messalina* (I); a *Rock* in *The Maid's Tragedy* (I); a *Scaffold* in *The Virgin Martyr* (IV), *Messalina* (V), a *Stake* in *The Martyred Soldier* (III).

ABOVE THE STAGE

The Tempest calls for *Solemne and strange Musicke: and Prosper on the top (invisible:)* (III.iii.16). In eleven other plays this space is referred to as *above* or *aloft*. *Poetaster* (IV.ix); *Catiline His Conspiracy* (III); *The Revenge of Bussy D'Ambois* (V); *The Virgin Martyr* (II.iii); *The Renegado* (III.v); *The Duchess of Suffolk* (II); *The Seven Champions of Christendom* (V); *Messalina* (III, V); *The Island Princess* (IV, V); *The Humorous Lieutenant* (III.iv); *Love and Honour* (V). It is referred to as *the walls* in two plays: *The Devil's Charter* (II.i); *The Maid's Tragedy* (V). It is referred to as *two windo's as out of two contiguous buildings* in *The Devil Is an Ass* (II.vi). *Juno descends* to "this grasse-plot" in *The Tempest* (IV.i.73). Actors *descend* to the stage in four other plays: *The Whore of Babylon* (Iv); *The Valiant Welshman* (I.ii); *The Seven Champions of Christendom* (I); *Messalina* (V).

DOORS OR HANGINGS

The Tempest has *Here Prospero discovers Ferdinand and Miranda, playing at Chesse* (V.i.171). An actor *opens the door* in *1 Arviragus and Philicia* (I) and *Messalina* (II); in *The Renegado* an actor *opens a doore* and later *lockes it* (II.v). In *The Island Princess* appears *Enter Armusa and his company breaking open a doore* (II), followed six lines later by *The King discover'd;* later *Armusa lockes the doore* (III).

An *arras, curtains,* or a *traverse* are drawn or parted in nine plays: *Antonio's Revenge* (I.iii, III.iv, V.v); *The Whore of Babylon* (A4v); *The Devil's Charter* (V.vi); *The Faithful Shepherdess* (V); *The Revenge of Bussy D'Ambois* (V); *The Valiant Welshman* (V.i); *The Duchess of Malfy* (IV.i); *The Rebellion* (I); *Love and Honour* (III). In *The Devil's Charter* an actor *discovereth his tent* (IV.iv). An actor is described as *in his study* in *The Devil's Charter* (I.iv, IV.i, V.vi) and *Catiline His Conspiracy* (I). *The Rebellion* has *sitting in a closet* (III). One finds *Fire flashing out of the study* in *The Virgin Martyr* (V). In *The Renegado* appears *A shop discoverde* (I.iii); in *The Knight of the Burning Pestle* is *Enter Rafe like a Grocer in's shop, with two Prentices Reading Palmerin of England* (I). In *The Humorous Lieutenant* an actor enters at *a Table, writing* (II.iii). *The Martyred Soldier* has *discovered sitting loaden with many Irons* (III). In *The Whore of Babylon* (G2v) a *Cave suddenly breakes open.* In *The Duchess of Malfy* (IV.ii) Bosola *Shewes the children strangled.*

6 Twelfth Night at the Middle Temple

At the conclusion of this attempt to correlate pictorial and architectural evidence concerning pre-Restoration stages with early texts of all the extant plays probably first performed by English professional actors in the years 1599–1642, it may be instructive to examine closely the earliest extant text of Shakespeare's *Twelfth Night* and to suggest how it may have been staged during Candlemas Feast 1601/2 at the Middle Temple. A record of this event is found in the *Diary* of John Manningham:

> Feby 2nd. At our feast we had a play called Twelfth Night or What you will, much like the Commedy of Errors or Menechmi in Plautus, but most like and neere to that in Italian called Inganni. A good practise in it to make the Steward beleeve his Lady Widdowe was in love with him by counterfeyting a letter from his Lady in generall termes, telling him what shee liked best in him and prescribing his gesture in smiling his apparaile etc., and then when he came to practise making him beleeve they tooke him to be mad.[1]

Manningham does not identify the actors, but it is improbable that the play was performed at this time by a company other than Shakespeare's. The King's men kept *Twelfth Night* in their active repertory and revived it at Court on Easter Monday 1618 and again on Candlemas 1622/3.[2]

Greg suggests that the promptbook, or a transcript of it, served as printer's copy for the First Folio text of *Twelfth Night*.[3] The following plot of the entrances and exits in this text shows that the action of the play is well suited for performance in front of an unlocalized screen with two doorways, such as those at the Middle Temple.[4] One doorway is designated as A, the other B.

My staging plot also observes a number of Elizabethan conventions. First, the obvious theatrical function of the screen is to keep the actors from the view of the audience until they enter, and to hide them from view when they *exeunt*. The direction "within" indicates the space behind the screen where actors are out of sight of, but may be heard by, the audience. This space may also serve as a tiring-house where actors change clothing. Second, the acting area in front of the screen is essentially *placeless*. For some scenes it may be given temporary localization by a dialogue reference, or by special properties brought on, but when the area is cleared of actors and properties at the end of a scene, any suggestion of place is nullified. And third, at the end of most scenes, actors *exeunt* together through one doorway, and almost immediately another group of actors enters through the other doorway to start the next scene. If the dialogue indicates that actors meet at the start of a scene, one enters through doorway A, the other through doorway B. If the dialogue indicates that actors part at the end of a scene, one exits through doorway A, the other through doorway B. And if an actor exits and re-enters during the same scene, he re-enters by the same doorway through which he made his exit.

Act and scene headings and all stage directions in the Folio text of *Twelfth Night* are cited verbatim in the following staging plot. Their position on each line also corresponds to that in the Folio. In brackets to the right of the text are my conjectures about the doorway used for each entrance and exit, as well as about other stage business required by the dialogue. At the right of the text are the line numbers given in *Twelfth Night,* ed. Arthur Quiller-Couch and John Dover Wilson, 2nd ed. (Cambridge: Cambridge University Press, 1949). As the line division in this edition does not always agree with the Folio, a few inconsistencies appear in my line numberings. Except for the stage directions immediately following act and scene headings, line numbers for stage directions are taken from the line immediately preceding. I cite all dialogue references to fictional locale and to actors' movements. The dialogue very seldom specifies the *place* of action but often gives *direction* to the actors' movements as they meet, part, lead, or follow. I cite all dialogue cues for exits even though most cues do not indicate the fictional place to which the actors go.

Twelfe Night, Or What You Will

Actus Primus, Scaena Prima.

Enter Orsino Duke of Illyria, Curio, and other
Lords. [A]

Duke. . . . How now what newes from her?	22
Enter Valentine. [B]	22
Valentine. So please my Lord, I might not be admitted,	23
Duke. . . . Away before me, to sweet beds of Flowres,	39
Love-thoughts lye rich, when canopy'd with bowres. *Exeunt [A]*	40

Scena Secunda.

Enter Viola, a Captaine, and Saylors. [B]

Viola. What Country (Friends) is this?	1
Captain. This is Illyria Ladie.	2
Viola. . . . Ile serve this Duke,	54
Thou shalt present me as an Eunuch to him,	55
Viola. I thanke thee: Lead me on. *Exeunt [A]*	63

Scaena Tertia.

Enter Sir Toby, and Maria. [B]

Toby. . . . for here coms	44
Sir *Andrew Agueface.*	
Enter Sir Andrew. [B]	
Maria. . . . I let go your hand, I am barren. *Exit Maria [B]*	81
Andrew. . . . Shall we sit about some Revels?	137

Toby. **No** sir, it is leggs and thighes: let me see thee ca-   141
per. Ha, higher: ha, ha, excellent.   *Exeunt [B]*   142

Scena Quarta.

Enter Valentine, and Viola in mans attire. [A]

Valentine. If the Duke continue these favours towards you   1
Cesario . . .   2

       Enter Duke, Curio, and Attendants. [A]   8
Viola. I thanke you: heere comes the Count.   9

Duke. Stand you a-while aloofe. [*Others stand apart*] *Cesario,*   12

. . . Be not deni'de accesse, stand at her doores,   15

. . . some foure or five attend him,   36

Viola. Ile do my best   41
To woe your Lady: [*aside*] yet a barrefull strife,   42
Who ere I woe, myselfe would be his wife.
Exeunt. [*Duke, Curio, and Valentine A, Viola and Attendants B*]   43

Scena Quinta.

Enter Maria, and Clowne. [B]

Maria. Nay, either tell me where thou has bin, or I will   1
not open my lippes so wide as a brissle may enter, in way   2
of thy excuse: my Lady will hang thee for thy absence.   3

Maria. . . . here comes my   29
Lady: make your excuse wisely, you were best.   [*Exit B*]   30
    Enter Lady Olivia, with Malvolio. [and attendants, A]   30

      Enter Maria. [B]   96

Maria. Madam, there is at the gate, a young Gentle-   97
man, much desires to speake with you.   98

Olivia. Who of my people hold him in delay?   102
Maria. Sir *Toby* Madam, your kinsman.   103
Olivia. Fetch him off I pray you, he speakes nothing but   104
madman: Fie on him [*Exit Maria, B*]. Go you *Malvolio;* if it be a suit 105
from the Count, I am sicke, or not at home. What you   106
will, to dismisse it.   *Exit Malvolio.* [*B*] 107

Clowne. . . . for heere he comes.   *Enter Sir Toby.* [*B*] 112
One of thy kin has a most weake *Pia-mater.*   113
Olivia. By mine honor halfe drunke. What is he at the   114
gate Cosin?   115
Toby. A Gentleman.   116

. . . Well, it's all one.   *Exit* [*A*] 129

Olivia. . . . go looke after him.   136
Clowne. He is but mad yet Madona, and the foole shall   137
looke to the madman.   [*Exit A*] 138
              Enter Malvolio. [*B*]   138
Malvolio. Madam, yond young fellow sweares hee will   139
speake with you.   140

Olivia. Let him approach: Call in my Gentlewoman.   162–3
Malvolio. Gentlewoman, my Lady calles.   *Exit* [*B*] 164–5
              Enter Maria. [*B*]   164–5
Olivia. Give me my vaile: come throw it ore my face, [*Maria does so*]
                                                                 166
Wee'l once more heare *Orsinos* Embassie.   167
              Enter Violenta. [*B*]   167

Olivia. Give us the place alone.   [*Exit Maria, B*] 222

. . . but we will draw the Curtain, and shew you the picture.   237
[*Unveils*] Looke you sir, such a one I was this present: Ist not well 238
done?   239

Get you to your Lord:	283
I cannot love him: let him send no more,	284
Unlesse (perchance) you come to me againe,	285
To tell me how he takes it: Fare you well:	286
I thanke you for your paines; spend this for mee. [Offers purse]	287
Viola. I am no feede poast, Lady; keepe your purse	288

. . . Farwell fayre crueltie. *Exit* [B]	292

Olivia. What hoa, *Malvolio.*	303
Enter Malvolio. [B]	303
Malvolio. Heere Madam, at your service.	303
Olivia. Run after that same peevish Messenger	304
The Countes man: he left this Ring behinde him [*gives ring*]	305

If that the youth will come this way to morrow,	309
Ile give him reasons for't: hie thee *Malvolio.*	310
Malvolio. Madam, I will. *Exit.* [B]	311

Olivia. What is decreed, must be: and be this so. [*Exit A*]	315

Finis, Actus primus.

Actus Secundus, Scaena prima.

Enter Antonio & Sebastian. [B]

Antonio. Will you stay no longer: nor will you not that	1
I go with you.	2
Sebastian. By your patience, no . . .	3

Sebastian. . . . I am	39
bound to the Count Orsino's Court, farewell. *Exit* [A]	40
Antonio. The gentlenesse of all the gods go with thee:	41
I have many enemies in Orsino's Court,	42
Else would I very shortly see thee there:	43
But come what may, I do adore thee so,	44
That danger shall seeme sport, and I will go. *Exit.* [A]	45

Scaena Secunda.

Enter Viola and Malvolio, at severall doores. [Viola A, Malvolio B]

Malvolio. Were you not ev'n now, with the Countesse *O-*   1
livia?   2
   Viola. Even now sir, on a moderate pace, I have since a-   3
riv'd but hither.   4
   Malvolio. She returnes this Ring to you (sir) you might   5
have saved mee my paines   6

. . . receive it so. [*Holds out ring*]   11
   Viola. She tooke the Ring of me [*?*] Ile none of it.   12

Malvolio. . . . If it bee worth stoo-   15
ping for, there it lies, [*throws down ring*] in your eye: if not, bee it his
                                                                    that   16
findes it.   *Exit.* [*B*]   17

   Viola. O time, thou must untangle this, not I,   40
It is too hard a knot for me t'unty.   [*Exit A*]   41

Scaena Tertia.

Enter Sir Toby, and Sir Andrew. [B]

Enter Clowne. [A]
Andrew. Heere comes the foole yfaith.   16

Clowne sings.   41

Catch sung   74
Enter Maria. [A]   74
Maria. What a catterwalling doe you keepe here? If   75
my Ladie have not call'd up her Steward *Malvolio,* and   76
bid him turne you out of doores, never trust me.   77

Enter Malvolio. [A]   90

Malvolio. . . . she shall know of it by this   129
hand.   *Exit* [A]   130

Maria. . . . For this night to bed, and   181
dreame on the event: Farewell.   *Exit* [A]   182

Toby. Come, come, Ile go burne some Sacke, tis too late   196
to go to bed now: Come knight, come knight.   *Exeunt* [B]   197

Scena Quarta.

Enter Duke, Viola, Curio, and others. [A]

Curio. Feste the Jester my Lord, a foole that the Ladie   11
Oliviaes Father tooke much delight in. He is about the   12
house.   13
Duke. Seeke him out, and play the tune the while.
                                    [*Exit Curio, B*]   14
                                    Musicke playes.

Enter Curio & Clowne. [B]   41

Duke. I prethee sing.   *Musicke.*   50

Duke. There's for thy paines. [*Gives coin*]   67

Clowne. . . . Farewell.   *Exit* [B]   78
Duke. Let all the rest give place . . .
                            [*Curio and others exeunt A*]   79

Viola. Sir, shall I to this Lady?   122
Duke. I that's the Theame,   123
To her in haste: give her this Jewell: say, [*gives jewel*]   124
My love can give no place, bide no denay.
                            exeunt [*Duke A, Viola B*]   125

Scena Quinta.

Enter Sir Toby, Sir Andrew, and Fabian. [B]

Toby. Come thy wayes Signior *Fabian.*	1
Fabian. Nay Ile come . . .	2

Enter Maria. [A]   13

Toby. Heere comes the little villaine: How now my   14
Mettle of India?   15
   Maria. Get ye all three into the box tree; *Malvolio's*   16
comming downe this walke, he has beene yonder i' the   17
Sunne practising behavior to his own shadow this halfe   18
houre: observe him for the love of Mockerie; for I know   19
this Letter wil make a contemplative Ideot of him. Close   20
in the name of jeasting, lye thou there: for heere comes   21
the Trowt, that must be caught with tickling.

                    Exit [A, after placing   22
                    letter on ground. Men
                    hide from Malvolio in
                    doorway B, but when they
                    speak, they are seen and
                    heard by the audience]

Enter Malvolio. [A]   23

Malvolio. What employment have we heere? [*Picks up letter*]   84

Malvolio. [*Reads*] *To the unknowne belov'd* . . .   94
     [*Comments by others interspersed to line 180*]
I thanke thee, I will smile, I wil do every thing that thou   181
wilt have me.   *Exit. [A]*

Enter Maria. [A]   188

Fabian. Nor I neither.   189
Toby. Heere comes my noble gull catcher.   190

Maria. If you will then see the fruites of the sport, mark   200
his first approach before my Lady   201

. . . if you wil   206
see it follow me.   207
    Toby. To the gates of Tartar, thou most excellent divell   208
of wit.   209
    Andrew. Ile make one too.   *Exeunt.* [A]   210
                        Finis Actus secundus.

Actus Tertius, Scaena prima.

Enter Viola and Clowne. [*Clown A, Viola B*]

Viola. Save thee Friend and thy Musick: dost thou live   1
by thy Tabor?   2

Viola. . . . Hold there's expences for thee. [*Gives coin*]   43

I understand you sir, tis well begg'd [*Gives another*]   54

    Clowne. . . . My Lady is within sir, I   56
will conster to them whence you come, who you are, and   57
what you would are out of my welkin, I might say Ele-   58
ment, but the word is over worne.   *exit* [A]   59

Enter Sir Toby and Andrew. [A]   68

    Toby. Will you incounter the house, my Neece is desi-   74
rous you should enter, if your trade be to her.   75

Enter Olivia, and Gentlewoman. [*Maria, A*]   84

Olivia. Let the Garden doore be shut, and leave mee to   92
my hearing. Give me your hand sir.   [*Exeunt Toby, Andrew,*
                       and Maria, B]   93

Clocke strikes. 131
Olivia. The clocke upbraides me with the waste of time: 132

Viola. And so adieu good Madam, never more, 163
Will I my Masters teares to you deplore. 164
Olivia. Yet come againe: for thou perhaps mayst move 165
That heart which now abhorres, to like his love. *Exeunt [Olivia A,*
Viola B] 166

Scoena Secunda.

Enter Sir Toby, Sir Andrew, and Fabian. [B]

Andrew. No faith, Ile not stay a jot longer: 1

Toby. Wee'l call thee at the Cubiculo: Go. *Exit Sir Andrew. [A]* 51

Enter Maria. [B] 63
Toby. Looke where the youngest Wren of mine comes. 64
Maria. If you desire the spleene, and will laughe your 65
selves into stitches, follow me . . . 66

Toby. Come bring us, bring us where he is. *Exeunt Omnes. [B]* 82

Scaena Tertia.

Enter Sebastian and Anthonio. [A]

Antonio. . . . hold sir, here's my purse, [*gives purse*] 37

Sebastian. Ile be your purse-bearer, and leave you 47
For an houre. 48
Antonio. To th'Elephant. 49
Sebastian. I do remember. *Exeunt. [Antonio A, Sebastian B]* 50

Scaena Quarta.

Enter Olivia and Maria. [A]

Olivia. I have sent after him, he sayes hee'l come: 1

. . . Where is *Malvolio?*   7
Maria. He's comming Madame: 8
But in a very strange manner. He is sure possest Madam.   9

Olivia. Go call him hither.   *[Exit Maria, A]* 14
            Enter Malvolio. [A, with Maria]   14

            Enter Servant. [A]   59
Servant. Madame, the young Gentleman of the Count   60
Orsino's is return'd, I could hardly entreate him backe: he   61
attends your Ladyships pleasure.   62
Olivia. Ile come to him.   *[Exit Servant, A]*   63
Good *Maria,* let this fellow be lookd too. Where's my   64
Cosine *Toby,* let some of my people have a speciall care   65
of him, I would not have him miscarrie for the halfe of   66
my Dowry.   *exit [A. Exit Maria, B]*   67

            Enter Toby, Fabian, and Maria. [B]   87
Toby. Which way is hee in the name of sanctity   88

Malvolio. . . you shall knowe more   128
heereafter.   *Exit [A]*   129

Toby. Come, wee'l have him in a darke room & bound.   139

. . . but see, but see.   145
            Enter Sir Andrew. [A]
Fabian. More matter for a May morning.   146
Andrew. Heere's the Challenge, reade it [*Shows paper*]   147

Toby. Give me. [*reads*]   151
Youth whatsoever thou art, thou art but a scurvy fellow.
            [*Comments by others interspersed to line 175*]

Go sir *Andrew:* scout mee for him at the corner   180
of the Orchard . . .   181

. . . Away.   186
   Andrew. Nay let me alone for swearing   *Exit [B]*   187

       Enter Olivia and Viola. [A]   199
   Fabian. Heere he comes with your Neece, give them way   200
till he take leave, and presently after him.   201
   Toby. I will meditate the while upon some horrid message   202
for a Challenge.   *[Exeunt Toby and Fabian, B]*   203

   Olivia. Well, come againe to morrow; far-thee-well,   219
A Fiend like thee might beare my soule to hell.   *[Exit A]* 220
       Enter Toby and Fabian. [B]   220

   Viola. I will returne againe into the house, and desire   243
some conduct of the Lady . . .   244

   Toby. . . . Backe you shall not to the house, unlesse you   249
undertake that with me, which with as much safetie you   250
might answer him . . .   251

   Viola. This is as uncivill as strange. I beseech you, doe   254
me this courteous office, as to know of the Knight what   255
my offence to him is . . .   256

   Toby. I will doe so. Signiour *Fabian,* stay you by this   258
Gentleman, till my returne.   *Exit Toby. [B]*   259

   Fabian. . . . will you walke towards him, I will make   269
your peace with him, if I can.   270
   Viola. I shall bee much bound to you for't: I am one,   271
that had rather go with sir Priest, then sir knight: I care   272
not who knowes so much of my mettle.   *Exeunt. [A]*   273
       Enter Toby and Andrew. [B]   273

   Toby. I but he will not now be pacified,   282
Fabian can scarse hold him yonder.   283

Enter Fabian and Viola. [*A*]   290

Toby. . . . Come on, too't.   307
Andrew. Pray God he keepe his oath. [Draws]   308
     Enter Antonio. [*A*]   308
Viola. I do assure you tis against my will. [Draws]   309
Antonio. Put up your sword: if this yong Gentleman   310
Have done offence, I take the fault on me: 311

Toby. Nay, if you be an undertaker, I am for you.
     [*Antonio and Toby draw*]   316
    Enter Officers. [*A*]   316
Fabian. O good sir *Toby* hold: heere come the Officers. 317-8
Toby. Ile be with you anon. [*Puts up sword*]   319
Viola. Pray sir, put your sword up if you please. [*Puts up sword*] 320
Andrew. Marry will I sir: and for that I promis'd you Ile 321
be as good as my word . . . [*Puts up sword, as does Antonio*] 322

Viola. . . . Hold, there's halfe my Coffer. [*Offers coins*]   345

1 Officer. The man growes mad, away with him:
Come, come sir.   369
Antonio. Leade me on. *Exit* [*A, following Officers*] 370

Toby. Come hither Knight, come hither *Fabian:* Weel
whisper ore a couplet or two of most sage sawes. [*They step aside*] 376

Viola. . . . Oh if it prove,   383
Tempests are kinde, and salt waves fresh in love. [*Exit A*] 384

Andrew. Slid, Ile after him againe, and beate him.   391
Toby. Do, cuffe him soundly, but never draw thy sword   392
Andrew. And I do not.   [*Exit A*]   393
Fabian. Come, let's see the event.   394
Toby. I dare lay any money, twill be nothing yet.
    · *Exit* [*Toby and Fabian, A*]   395

Actus Quartus, Scaena prima.

Enter Sebastian and Clowne. [B]

Clowne. Will you make me beleeve, that I am not sent for   1
you?   2

Sebastian. I prethee foolish greeke depart from me, there's   17
money for thee, [*gives coin*] if you tarry longer, I shall give worse   18
paiment.   19

          Enter Andrew, Toby and Fabian. [A]   22
Andrew. Now sir, Have I met you again: ther's for you.
                    [*Strikes at Sebastian*] 23
Sebastian. Why there's for thee, and there, and there,
                   [*strikes Andrew*] 24–5
Are all the people mad?   26
   Toby. Hold sir, or Ile throw your dagger ore the house.
                  [*Seizes Sebastian*] 27–8
Clowne. This will I tell my Lady straight . . .   [*Exit A*] 29

Sebastian. I will be free from thee. What wouldst [thou] now?
                  [*Frees self*] 40–41
If thou dar'st tempt me further, draw thy sword. [*Draws*]   42
   Toby. What, what? [Draws] Nay then I must have an Ounce or 43
two of this malapert blood from you.   44
           Enter Olivia. [A]   44
Olivia. Hold, *Toby*, on thy life I charge thee hold.   45
Toby. Madam. [*Both men put up swords*]   46

Olivia. . . . Rudesby be gone.
        [*Exeunt Toby, Andrew, and Fabian, B*] 51

Olivia. Nay come I prethee, would thoud'st be rul'd by me.   64–5
Sebastian. Madam, I will.   66
Olivia. O say so, and so be.   *Exeunt [A]* 67

Scaena Secunda.

Enter Maria and Clowne. [B]

Maria. Nay, I prethee put on this gown, & this beard,	1
make him beleeve thou art sir *Topas* the Curate, doe it	2
quickly. Ile call sir *Toby* the whilst. [*Exit B*]	3

Clowne. . . . The Competitors enter.   10
                   Enter Toby. [B, with Maria]   10

                  Malvolio within. [to end of scene] 24
Malvolio. Who cals there?   25

Toby. To him in thine owne voyce, and bring me word   67
how thou findst him . . .

. . . Come by and by to my Chamber.   *Exit [B, with Maria]* 72

Clowne. I will fetch you light, and paper, and inke.   118
Malvolio. Foole, Ile requite it in the highest degree: 119
I prethee be gone.   120

Clowne. Adieu good man divill.   *Exit [A]* 130

Scaena Tertia.

Enter Sebastian. [B, Solus]

. . . Where's *Anthonio* then,   4
I could not finde him at the Elephant,   5

. . . But heere the Lady comes.   21
               Enter Olivia, and Priest. [A]   21

Olivia. . . . Now go with me, and with this holy man   23
Into the Chantry by . . .   24

Olivia. Then lead the way good father, & heavens so shine,   34

That they may fairely note this acte of mine.   *Exeunt.* [B] 35

                     Finis Actus Quartus.

Actus Quintus. Scena Prima.

Enter Clowne and Fabian. [A]

Fabian. Now as thou lov'st me, let me see his Letter   1

Clowne. Do not desire to see this Letter.   5

       Enter Duke, Viola, Curio, and Lords. [A]   7

Duke. Belong you to the Lady *Olivia,* friends?   8

Clowne. I sir, we are some of her trappings.   9

Duke. Thou shalt not be the worse for me, there's gold.

              [Gives coin to Clowne] 27

Duke. . . . there's another. *[Gives another]*   35

Duke. . . . if you will let your Lady know I am here to speak   41

with her, and bring her along with you, it may awake my   42

bounty further.   43

Clowne. . . . let your bounty take a nappe, I will awake it   47

anon.   *Exit* [B, *with Fabian*] 48

       Enter Anthonio and Officers. [A]   48

Viola. Here comes the man sir, that did rescue mee.   49

       Enter Olivia and attendants. [B]   95

Duke. Heere comes the Countesse . . .   96

Duke. . . . Take him aside. *[Officers take Antonio aside]*   99

Olivia. Call forth the holy Father.   *[Exit Attendant, B]* 141

Enter Priest. [B]   148

Olivia. O welcome Father: 149

Enter Sir Andrew. [B]   170

Andrew. For the love of God a Surgeon, send one pre-   171
sently to sir *Toby.*   172

Enter Toby and Clowne. [B, with Fabian]   187

Andrew. Heere comes sir *Toby* halting, you shall heare more . . .

                                                            189

Olivia. Get him to bed, and let his hurt be look'd too.
            [Exeunt Toby, Andrew, Clowne, and Fabian, A]   207
                     Enter Sebastian. [B]   207
Sebastian. I am sorry Madam I have hurt your kinsman: 208

Enter Clowne with a Letter, and Fabian. [A]   279

Olivia. Open't, and read it.   287
Clowne. Looke then to be well edified, when the Foole   288
delivers the Madman. *[Reads] By the Lord Madam.*   289

Olivia. Read it you, sirrah. *[Takes letter from Clown,*
                          gives it to Fabian]   300
Fabian. Reads. By the Lord Madam, you wrong me . . .   301

Olivia. See him deliver'd *Fabian,* bring him hither.
                             [Exit Fabian, A]   315

Enter Malvolio. [A, with Fabian]   326

Malvolio. Lady you have, pray you peruse that Letter.
                          [Shows letter to Olivia]   330

Malvolio. Ile be reveng'd on the whole packe of you *[!]   [Exit A]* 377

Duke. Pursue him, and entreate him to a peace

                                        [*Exit Fabian, A*]   379

Duke. But when in other habites you are seene,   386
Orsino's Mistris, and his fancies Queene.   *Exeunt* [*B, except Clown*]   387
                          Clowne sings.   387

And wee'l strive to please you every day.   [*Exit B*]   407

FINIS.

Appendices
Notes
Index

Appendix A.
Major Scholarship since 1940

An appraisal is offered here of fourteen books on Shakespearean stagecraft published since 1940. The examination is not intended to discredit what are often useful and illuminating works of scholarship. Instead, it is meant to show how scholars applying different criteria for the evaluation of evidence can arrive at widely divergent and sometimes mutually contradictory conclusions. The works discussed are indebted to the following pioneer stage studies: Joseph Quincy Adams, *Shakespearean Playhouses* (Boston: Houghton Mifflin, 1917); Victor E. Albright, *The Shakespearian Stage* (New York: Columbia University Press, 1909); Muriel C. Bradbrook, *Elizabethan Stage Conditions* (Cambridge: Cambridge University Press, 1932); William J. Lawrence, *The Elizabethan Playhouse and Other Studies* (Stratford-upon-Avon: Shakespeare Head Press, 1912); Lawrence, *Pre-Restoration Stage Studies* (Cambridge: Harvard University Press, 1927); Lawrence, *Those Nut-Cracking Elizabethans* (London: Argonaut Press, 1935); Ashley H. Thorndike, *Shakespeare's Theater* (New York: Macmillan, 1916). A useful bibliography appears in Charles T. Prouty, ed., *Studies in the Elizabethan Stage* (Hamden, Conn.: Shoe String Press, 1961), which cites 116 books and articles. In the same volume an article by James Stinson, "Reconstructions of Elizabethan Playhouses," pp. 55–124, summarizes the findings of, and reprints illustrations from, several studies offering hypothetical reconstructions.

Six important books place primary emphasis on one or more contemporary illustrations, but none of them cites the available playhouse promptbooks and other dramatic manuscripts. George R. Kernodle, *From Art to Theatre* (Chicago: Chicago University Press, 1944), reproduces early pictures of *tableaux vivants,* triumphal arches, and municipal theaters in England and on the Continent. From these he reconstructs a stage placed in front of an elaborate façade with the following main features: a pair of heavy doors that swing open center stage to provide a discovery space, two smaller entrance doors on either side of the center door, a small window above each of the small entrance doors, and a curtained upper stage above the center doors (Fig. 47, p. 152). Although Kernodle makes a few textual references, he does not attempt to show how often or in which plays this configuration of stage equipment would be required in actual performance by professional actors.

Glynne Wickham, *Early English Stages,* Volume II, Part i (New York: Columbia University Press, 1963), concludes with a study of the Swan, built in 1596. After a survey of architectural precedents for Elizabethan playhouse design, Wickham accepts DeWitt's sketch of the Swan "at its face value without modification, interpolation or any other unwarranted change. . . . The whole of this stage, with its screen, gallery and dressing-room, indistinguishable from that of the Tudor Hall, is set down, put, placed, dumped in the conventional three-tiered Tudor game-house in a manner which will admit the maximum number of spectators consistent with box-office capacity and a reasonable view of the action on the stage" (p. 204). Among Wickham's many valuable contributions to an understanding of theatrical conditions of this period are his cogent arguments against the "Inn Yard" theory about Elizabethan performances and his suggestion that "a hall or gallery within the inn was in fact the theatre" (p. 188). He reproduces the Trinity Hall drawing and cites Prouty's article, but he does not discuss Prouty's suggestion about how this structure might be fitted with hangings for performance. Wickham points to the difficulties in drawing inferences about staging from printed playbooks (p. 154), but he does not discuss the available playhouse documents.

C. Walter Hodges, *The Globe Restored,* rev. ed. (New York: Coward-McCann, 1968), offers an abundantly illustrated summary of pictorial evidence concerning early theatrical performances in England and on the Continent. He suggests that the basic equipment for the Elizabethan public stage was developed from the trestle platform and portable booth used by earlier strolling players. In Shakespeare's time a stage and curtained booth were set up against the tiring-house façade of the playhouse. The booth was used for the discovery of actors, or properties, or both; its top was boarded over, and this space could provide an acting place "above." As already shown, the staging needs of most plays first acted in the years 1599–1642 can be met by curtains hung from a gallery or placed over open doorways. To be sure, a curtained booth would provide a suitable "within" or backstage area for performances out-of-doors or at an acting place lacking doorways or gallery, but otherwise it would not be needed.

Richard Southern, *The Open Stage* (London: Faber & Faber, 1953), offers eloquent arguments for performing the plays of Shakespeare and his contemporaries on a *placeless* open stage rather than with representational settings in the "picture frame" stage found in most conventional modern theaters (p. 47). Southern supports his case by reference to the Swan drawing, but he makes very few textual references.

Another proponent of the open stage and of flexibility in Elizabethan staging procedures is J. L. Styan, whose *Shakespearean Stagecraft* (Cambridge: Cambridge University Press, 1967) provides a valuable study of Shakespeare's visual and aural stagecraft. In general, Styan accepts the authenticity of the Swan drawing, but his comments about Shakespeare's stage equipment are limited to what "has already been advanced by scholars of the Elizabethan theatre" (p. vii). Styan states his textual evidence is *The New Shakespeare* of Arthur Quiller-Couch and John Dover Wilson (Cambridge: Cambridge University Press).

A. M. Nagler, *Shakespeare's Stage* (New Haven: Yale University Press, 1958), suggests that the Swan drawing represents a rehearsal, which is the reason hangings are not shown. He reconstructs a "Shakespearean stage" from the basic frame of the Swan façade, to which is added a pavilion or "tent" such as that mentioned in Thomas Platter's letter describing a performance of a play at Bishopsgate in 1599, free-standing properties such as those listed in the Henslowe papers, and the back cloth mentioned in records of Court performances: "The two doors of the [Swan] tiring-house cannot be seen during the performance: they are covered by a curtain, which hangs from the gallery and has three openings. Before both doors there are slits in the curtain; the third opening is not visible, for in front of it stands the pavilion which extends up to the gallery. The tent itself is closed off with curtains" (p. 53). Nagler then describes how *Romeo and Juliet* may have been first performed with this equipment. Though it is true that the play could have been so acted, questions remain as to how much of this stage equipment was required or actually used. Nagler's book concludes with a reconstruction of a performance of *The Tempest* at Blackfriars, probably under essentially the same conditions as *Romeo and Juliet* at the public theater.

If studies that rely on pictorial evidence disagree about Shakespearean stagecraft, there is an even greater disparity in the conclusions reached by scholars who rely for the most part on textual evidence. Most scholars in the latter group either ignore part of the pictorial evidence or try to set it aside because it does not support the conclusions drawn from the texts. There are, however, serious inconsistencies in their criteria for the evaluation of textual evidence. Certain obviously important questions about each text should be answered as fully as possible: what evidence is there to indicate the place and date of performance of the play before 1642, what is the date of the text, and is there any evidence that it may be dependent on a promptbook or transcript therefrom? A fair and logical way of evaluating the findings of earlier studies is to examine their answers to these questions. It turns out that some theories about Shakespearean staging are based on textual evidence of doubtful validity.

Among the proponents of the controversial "multiple stage" theory is John Cranford Adams, whose *The Globe Playhouse: Its Design and Equipment,* 2nd ed. (New York: Barnes and Noble, 1961) offers evidence for the hypothetical scale model reconstruction of the Globe on display at the Folger Shakespeare Library. In his Preface Adams states:

> This study was based primarily on two assumptions: the first that the requirements of Elizabethan plays—requirements both explicit and implicit—necessarily reflect the design, equipment, and conventions of the stages for which they were written: and the second that as far as possible *all* the evidence should be taken into account inasmuch as studies based primarily upon pictorial evidence and stage directions, or upon the plays of one dramatist, one theatre, or even one period have failed to yield satisfactory results (pp. vii–viii).

Although Adams accepts some structural features of the Swan drawing, he finds that it "abounds in . . . contradictions . . . and obvious errors" (p. 49), the most conspicuous being the lack of a curtain before an inner stage (p. 136). With some reservations he accepts the *Roxana* and *Messalina* drawings and suggests that they are intended to "represent the public unroofed type of stage" (p. 94). Adams therefore uses these drawings to support his theories about a rear stage at the Globe.

In Chapter VI, "The Tiring-House, First Level," Adams advances an hypothesis concerning the "rear stage": "Elizabethan actors needed a supplementary, shallow rear stage suitable for use (1) as a three-dimensional back-drop when the two stages were merged into one large interior . . . (2) as an interior logically connected with a larger exterior . . . and (3) as in itself an interior" (p. 173). But in an important subsection entitled "The Hangings in the Rear Wall of the Study" (pp. 181–191), Adams cites stage directions of four plays that were probably not acted before 1642, if indeed they were ever acted. These include *The Jew's Tragedy* by William Hemminges, first printed in 1662, about which Bentley states, "There is no evidence of the existence of *The Jews' Tragedy* before the closing of the theatres, and W. W. Greg seems to doubt that it had been composed before the beginning of the wars" (IV, 547); *Andromana* by "J. S.," described by Adams as "written 1641?" but which was first printed in 1660 and about which Bentley maintains, "The precise date of *Andromana* cannot be set, but an allusion in III.5 makes it clear that it was written after the closing of the theatres. . . There is no evidence that *Andromana* itself was ever performed, and the handling of the material as well as the date suggest that it is closet drama" (V, 1034–1035); Sir William Davenant's *Albovine*, which was first printed in 1629 but about which Bentley concludes, "it seems fairly clear that the play was never acted" (III, 198); and Leonard Willan's *Orgula*, which is listed as "Unacted?" by Harbage for 1658, the year of its first printing.

This eclectic choice of plays could perhaps be defended on the grounds that all the evidence should be taken into account, if in fact Adams did give all the evidence. This is not the case, however. A study of the titles listed in his index shows that he does not make even passing reference to fifty-nine plays for which there is reliable evidence of performance before 1642, but whose texts do not require or even suggest the use of a "rear stage" and which could be acted on the stages shown in the pictorial evidence.

Irwin Smith, *Shakespeare's Globe Playhouse: A Modern Reconstruc-*

tion (New York: Charles Scribner's Sons, 1956), agrees with Adams's appraisal of the Swan drawing and states that some of its details are "open to suspicion, as for instance the absence of any curtained aperture between the stage doors, and of any forward reaching stage-cover from which celestial descents could be made" (pp. 47–48). Smith suggests that the *Messalina* engraving was a poor copy of the *Roxana* drawing published eight years earlier. He further comments: "In neither case . . . do we know what sort of stage—whether public, private, or academic—the engravings represent; but in both cases the lack of any lighting apparatus, if it be granted full importance, seems to point to an outdoor stage" (p. 49).

Smith supports the multiple stage theory and acknowledges his debt to earlier work by Adams:

> His reconstruction of the Globe is as nearly complete and accurate as present-day scholarship is likely to produce . . . [but] my own studies have in a few instances led me to adopt theories at variance with his, less in respect to the design of the Globe's stages than in respect to their use. . . I have chosen to relate the use of the stages to the plays of Shakespeare, and to draw my illustrations from his plays, in preference to those of other less known and less accessible dramatists (pp. xv–xvi).

In his analysis of the action of Shakespeare's plays, Smith attempts to show how this hypothetical reconstruction may have provided a suitable stage setting. Concerning the "rear stage" he states:

> The special value of the rear stage lay in these three things: (1) by virtue of the fact that it was itself a walled-in area, it could serve appropriately to represent a room or other enclosure; (2) because it could be concealed from the audience by curtains, it could be fitted out with properties and wall hangings to give color and to suggest a definite locality; and (3) because it lay at the rear of the outer stage, it could be used in combination with the platform, either as a single large stage or as two separate but related stages, and by its setting could give localization to the two together (p. 106).

Smith's book concludes with the following statement: "In a thousand facets Shakespeare's plays reflect the conditions of the Globe stage, the stage which he inherited and which he helped to create. If Shakespeare's stage had been other than it was, Shakespeare's plays would be other than they are. Whatever the stage, they would still be works of towering genius, but they would not be the plays that we have today" (p. 197).

However, an examination of the textual evidence adduced by Smith to support his hypothetical reconstruction shows that his treatment of historical problems is perfunctory at best. He offers the following limited statement about where and when Shakespeare's plays were actually performed:

> Contemporary records of various sorts indicate that the Globe staged performances of *The Taming of the Shrew, Love's Labour's Lost, Romeo and Juliet, Richard II, Othello, Macbeth, Pericles, The Winter's Tale,* and *Henry VIII;* others, less explicit, imply Globe performances of *Julius Caesar, Troilus and Cressida, King Lear* and *Cymbeline.* As to the other plays in the canon no direct evidence exists. Even so, however, there can be little doubt that all the plays written by Shakespeare during the great decade from 1599 (when the Globe was built) to 1609 (when the King's Men began to act at Blackfriars also) were first presented on the Globe's stage. In addition to some of the plays already mentioned, they included *As You Like It, Twelfth Night, Hamlet, The Merry Wives of Windsor, All's Well That Ends Well, Measure for Measure, Antony and Cleopatra* and *Coriolanus* (pp. 11–12).

Although Smith points to the lack of "direct evidence" for the performance of some of Shakespeare's plays at the Globe, nowhere in his book does he acknowledge that seventeen of Shakespeare's plays are known to have been performed at places other than the Globe before 1642.

Smith offers a hypothetical reconstruction of another important Shakespearean playhouse in *Shakespeare's Blackfriars Playhouse: Its History and Its Design* (New York: New York University Press, 1964). Concerning the stage, Smith states: "No contemporary drawing or description of the Blackfriars stage is known to exist. In the absence of any direct information as to its design and equipment, we can reconstruct it only by analyzing the demands made upon the stage by the plays performed upon it, and so recognizing the physical resources that enabled the stage to meet those demands" (p. 210). On the basis of a wide variety of external and internal evidence, Smith compiles a list of 133 titles that he describes as the repertories of the Chapel-Revels children and the King's men at Blackfriars. Stage directions and allusions in the dialogue of these plays serve as the basis for his theories about stage equipment discussed in the final three chapters: "The Platform," "The Rear Stage," and "The Upper Stages." Smith's illustrations for the ground plan and elevation of his reconstruction follow the general pattern he had earlier suggested for the Globe.

As in his study of the Globe, however, Smith does not give specific information about places and dates of performances for each play on his list, nor does he give the dates of the texts he cites. For example, two of Smith's most important pieces of evidence concerning a "curtained rear stage" are taken from *The Parson's Wedding*, listed in his repertory as by "Thomas Killigrew: 1639–40," and from *News from Plymouth*, listed as by "William Davenant: 1635." At first glance his evidence seems convincing:

> From *The Parson's Wedding* (V.ii): *The fiddlers play in the tiring-room; and the stage curtains are drawn, and discover a chamber, as it were, with two beds, and the ladies asleep in them; Mr. Wild being at Mrs. Pleasant's bed-side, and Mr. Careless at the Widow's* (p. 345).
>
> From *News from Plymouth* (IV.ii): *A Curtain drawn by Dash (his clerk) Trifle discover'd in his Study, Papers, Taper, Scale and Wax before him. Bell* (p. 346).

But closer study reveals that important historical and bibliographical scholarship has been ignored. For example, although allusions in the text of *The Parson's Wedding* suggest the author may have originally intended that this play be performed at Blackfriars, the work was not printed until 1663 and its title page states: "Written At Basil in Switzerland" (Bentley, IV, 703). The earliest extant record of performance is a notation by the Master of the Revels for 1663–64, indicating that the play may have been licensed during these years. In his *Diary*, Pepys (11 October 1664) refers to this play as being acted by the King's company. Since Killigrew, the author of the play, was manager of this company at the time the work was printed, it seems more than likely that the first edition reflects stage conditions of the Restoration playhouse rather than of Blackfriars over twenty years earlier.

News from Plymouth was first printed in the Davenant folio of 1673. Besides its late printing, this text offers further difficulties. The play was licensed for performance on 1 August 1635. At this time the King's men would have been playing at the Globe instead of at Blackfriars, which is confirmed by allusions in the Prologue. Furthermore, the Epilogue of the play, as Bentley observes, contains a dozen or more alterations that suggest the work was revised for revival during the Commonwealth or Restoration periods (III, 209–210). In the later period the play would most likely have been acted by the Duke of York's men, of which Davenant was the manager from 1660 to 1668. Thus, there is conflicting evidence concerning the playhouse at which the 1673 text of *News from Plymouth* may have been performed, but none of this evidence points to Blackfriars.

The index to Smith's book shows that *The Parson's Wedding* and *News from Plymouth* are cited a total of twenty-five times to support his theories about the stage at Blackfriars. In contrast to his reliance on these late printed texts, Smith gives only passing notice to four of the extant manuscript promptbooks from the repertory of the King's men: *Believe As You List, The Honest Man's Fortune, The Second Maiden's Tragedy,* and *Sir John van Olden Barnavelt;* these four texts are cited a total of twenty-two times. Smith lists these plays in the repertory of the King's men, but he does not identify them as playhouse manuscripts, nor does he discuss their textual characteristics. Yet these contemporary documents clearly provide a higher order of evidence than plays surviving only in late printed texts.

Although Smith cites thirty of the thirty-four plays first printed in the Beaumont and Fletcher Folio of 1647, he makes no reference to an important earlier study by R. C. Bald, who gives careful consideration to the nature of the copy that may lie behind the texts in this volume. Bald finds that many of the Folio texts carry markings that are probably related to prompt copy, while others do not (Bald, *Folio,* passim). His bibliographical research is clearly relevant to a discussion of staging methods by the King's men. See T. J. King, Review Article in *RenD,* 9:291–309(1966).

The multiple stage theory supported by Adams and Smith is contradicted by Leslie Hotson, whose *The First Night of Twelfth Night* (London: Hart-Davis, 1954) contends that Shakespeare's plays were performed with the audience surrounding the stage on four sides and the players making their entrances from individual "houses" or "mansions" set about the stage. Although it is true that references are found to canvas houses for performances at Court, where they may have been used for the precisely localized plays of Plautus and Terence or their Renaissance imitators, such equipment is neither required nor desirable in Shakespeare's plays, where most scenes are only vaguely localized.

Hotson claims to describe the staging of *Twelfth Night* at Whitehall on 6 January 1600/1, but this assignment of place and date of performance is highly conjectural. Nagler in *Shakespeare's Stage* raises serious objections to Hotson's interpretation of contemporary documents (p. 11). Furthermore, Hotson does not mention that the earliest external evidence for performance of this play is an entry in the *Diary* of John Manningham, who saw it acted at the Middle Temple on 2 February 1601/2, probably in the entertainment hall, of which there is now standing an exact replica of the bomb-damaged original built in 1574. Nor does Hotson mention that the play was not printed until 1623, probably from a manuscript dependent on prompt copy. As shown, the 1623 Folio text of *Twelfth Night* can be staged in any hall or playhouse with two entrances to the acting area.

Hotson's more recent work, *Shakespeare's Wooden O* (New York: Macmillan, 1960), offers an extension of his earlier theory, which he summarizes as follows:

> 1. Pageant-production was in the round, to an audience stationed on both sides, divided by an oblong stage.
> 2. The tiring-house or dressing room was underneath, inside the hollow stage.
> 3. The scenic axis was *transverse:* the "houses" stood facing each other from the stage ends. Access to them was up through traps (p. 281).

Here Hotson relies on textual evidence not clearly identified. His leading illustrative example is Middleton's *A Game at Chess,* performed at the Globe on nine consecutive days in August 1624, but he does not specify which of the nine variant texts—three quartos and six manuscripts—he cites. There is thus no way of determining the textual source for statements such as "Act 4 presents the dumb show of the 'wrong bedrooms' . . . with four separate places convincingly represented" (p. 44). Of all nine texts, the one probably closest to prompt copy—but not mentioned by Hotson—is the Archdale manuscript (Folger v.a. 231), dated 13 August 1624 and in the hand of Ralph Crane, scrivener for the King's men at the Globe. In this text the action of the dumb show is described as follows: "Musick. Dumb shew (brackets) Enter Black Queens Pawn wth Lights, conducting White Queens Pawne to a Chamber: and then ye Black Bishops Pawne to an other & ex[it]." The opening stage direction for Act One in this MS also reads: "Enter (from ye Black-house) a Woman-Pawne (in Black) & (from the White-house) a Woman-Pawne (in White)." The exchange described in the dumb show can be staged with two doorways as follows: Black Queen's Pawn enters from the White doorway with White Queen's Pawn, who is led across stage to the Black doorway, from which Black Bishop's Pawn is led across stage to the White doorway and *exeunt*. There is no textual evidence that "four separate places are convincingly represented."

Hotson's conjectures about the De Witt sketch are in keeping with his "in the round" theory. He interprets the vertical lines beneath the stage as representing "alleys . . . to give light to the end windows of the understage tiring-house or cellarage" and further states: "Trained to the one-side or façade stage of the Rederijkers, De Witt is struck by the Roman form of the *amphiteatra*, and, neglecting the rest of the house, comments pointedly and graphically by showing the audience in the lords' room on the other side of the Swan stage" (p. 91). His index shows no references to the other graphic or architectural evidence (p. 111).

George F. Reynolds, *The Staging of Elizabethan Plays at the Red Bull Theater, 1605–1625* (New York: Modern Language Association, 1940), carefully sets forth the historical evidence concerning plays performed at the Red Bull. He lists thirteen "A" plays that "we have good reason to believe were given at the Red Bull in the years we are concerned with," eighteen "B" plays that "were probably, but not surely, given at the Red Bull," and thirteen "C" plays "only possibly connected with the Red Bull in the years in question" (p. 5). Reynolds's conclusions are less dogmatic than those of most other scholars. He makes a good suggestion about a curtained framework added to the bare façade of the Swan, which would reconcile the seemingly divergent pictorial evidence (pp. 131–132).

Like Reynolds, Bernard Beckerman in *Shakespeare at the Globe, 1599–1609* (New York: Macmillan, 1962), is more cautious than Adams, Smith, or Hotson in his assertions about the facilities needed for production at the Globe:

Based solely on the evidence of the Globe plays, what then is the picture of the Globe stage? The principal part of the stage was a large rectangular platform upon which rested two pillars. At the rear of the platform two doors and a curtained recess between them provided access to the stage. The recess, which was an integral part of the tiring-house, had to accommodate less than half a dozen people. Above the recess and/or doors was an upper level principally required where characters related themselves to others below. In the floor of the outer stage there was at least one substantial trap. No machinery for flying either actors or properties existed (p. 106).

Beckerman notes the absence of curtains or hangings in the Swan drawing and states that this stage "could not have accommodated the Globe plays" (p. 100). As shown, however, hangings are not required in the following eight plays (listed with date of first printing): *Henry the Fifth* (1600), *King Lear* (1608), *Othello* (1622), *As You Like It* (1623), *Cymbeline* (1623), *Julius Caesar* (1623), *Measure for Measure* (1623), and *Twelfth Night* (1623). In those plays for which hangings are required, they are used in only one scene and would not necessarily be a permanent part of the stage structure.

Beckerman states that the bulk of his study is based on the evidence provided by the scripts of fifteen Shakespearean and fourteen non-Shakespearean plays that were presumably first produced at the Globe in the years between 1599 and 1609. His later time limit is chosen because after that date Blackfriars became the leading playhouse for the King's men. He does not point out, however, that nine of the fifteen Shakespearean plays cited were not published until the Folio of 1623; of these *Twelfth Night, Measure for Measure,* and *As You Like It* were performed at places other than the Globe before first printing.

Another problem with Beckerman's choice of textual evidence is that he does not take into account the work of bibliographical and textual scholars who attempt to determine the nature of the printer's copy used in setting type for playbooks of the period. For example, Beckerman cites *Timon of Athens* as evidence for a discovery space at the Globe, but as already shown, Greg observes that the Folio text of this play was probably printed from foul papers, a text not acted before printing. Although it is true that Beckerman's conclusions about the stage at the Globe would not be materially altered by the exclusion of *Timon* from his evidence, his findings would have greater authority if he had placed primary emphasis on texts more closely related to actual production.

My observations about these earlier studies and the conflicting theories they advance are intended to demonstrate the need for an examination of all the textual and historical evidence available rather than a few texts selected to support *a priori* assumptions. A useful corrective to a number of preconceptions is provided by Alfred Harbage, whose published Alexander Lectures at the University of Toronto, *Theatre for Shakespeare* (Toronto: University of Toronto Press, 1955), demonstrate once more his rare combination of erudition and theatrical sense. Having studied the original editions, he summarizes "the stage directions and implied action in eighty-six plays, including seventeen by Shakespeare— all those known to have been staged by particular companies using London amphitheatres between 1576, when the first was built, and 1608, when Shakespeare's company ceased using such structures exclusively, barring only such plays as were not printed within the same period" (p. 24). From this large body of evidence Harbage can generalize about rules rather than exceptions in Elizabethan staging procedures:

> The suburbs of the Elizabethan stage have received more emphasis than the stage itself. The extent of the over-emphasis is suggested by the following figures. In the eighty-six plays . . . forty-eight require no use of the gallery, thirty-nine no use of enclosure whether on or at the rear of the stage, and twenty-five no use of either gallery or enclosure. . . . In 1312 [of a total of 1463] scenes, the staging consisted of actors entering upon and leaving an open platform, either totally bare or equipped incidentally with a few seats, a table, a bed, a gibbet, a judgment bar, a raised throne, or the like. The exigencies of the fable dictated departures from the norm of simple platform playing (pp. 31–32).

These findings for the years 1576–1608 agree in substance with my own findings for the period 1599–1642, which suggests that the basic mode of production for professional actors did not change significantly after the King's men first acted at Blackfriars.

In this appraisal of stage scholarship, special mention should be made of work by Richard Hosley, nine of whose articles are cited in my notes. I hope I have clearly indicated the extent to which my work is indebted to his excellent analyses of pictorial and architectural evidence. Furthermore, in an important study, "The Use of the Upper Stage in *Romeo and Juliet," SQ,* 5: 371–379 (1954), Hosley demonstrates the significance of discriminating between a text that probably reflects actual performance procedures and one that probably does not. He states: "The important point is that Q1 [1597] (although printed two years earlier than Q2) represents our play *after* production and therefore may reflect production alterations necessary to stage the foul-papers text (represented by Q2) in an Elizabethan public theater" (p. 372, n. 13).

Appendix B.
Plays First Printed 1600–1659
Which Are Not Included

Greg lists 197 other plays first printed in the years 1600–1659, which are not included as evidence for this study either because they were probably first performed before late 1599, or because evidence is lacking or inconclusive concerning their performance by a professional company in the years 1599–1642. These works are listed chronologically below, with their Greg reference number, year of first printing, and reference works summarizing the available historical evidence.

Old Fortunatus	162	1600	Chambers, III, 290–291
The Maid's Metamorphosis	164	1600	Chambers, IV, 29
2 Henry the Fourth	167	1600	Chambers, *WS*, I, 377–384
Much Ado about Nothing	168	1600	Chambers, *WS*, I, 384–388
The Wisdom of Doctor Dodypoll	169	1600	Chambers, IV, 54
A Midsummer-Night's Dream	170	1600	Chambers, *WS*, I, 356–363
The Weakest Goeth to the Wall	171	1600	Chambers, IV, 52–53
The Merchant of Venice	172	1600	Chambers, *WS*, I, 368–375
Summer's Last Will and Testament	173	1600	Chambers, III, 451–453
Look about You	174	1600	Chambers, IV, 28
Every Man in His Humour	176	1600	Chambers, III, 359–360
Love's Metamorphosis	178	1601	Chambers, III, 416

133

The Downfall of Robert Earl of Huntingdon	179	1601	Chambers, III, 446–447
The Death of Robert Earl of Huntingdon	180	1601	Chambers, III, 447
Two Lamentable Tragedies	182	1601	Chambers, III, 518
Il Pastor Fido	183	1602	Chambers, IV, 40–41
Antonio and Mellida	184	1602	Chambers, III, 429–430
Darius	196	1603	Chambers, III, 209
Philotus	199	1603	Chambers, IV, 41
Doctor Faustus	205	1604	Chambers, III, 422–424
The Wit of a Woman	206	1604	Chambers, IV, 54
Croesus	209	1604	Chambers, III, 209
The Trial of Chivalry (This Gallant Cavaliero Dick Bowyer)	210	1605	Chambers, IV, 50–51
King Leir (Anonymous)	213	1605	Chambers, IV, 25–26
Captain Thomas Stukeley	220	1605	Chambers, IV, 47
I Jeronimo	221	1605	Chambers, IV, 22–23
The London Prodigal	222	1605	Chambers, IV, 27–28
The Return from Parnassus (The Scourge of Simony)	225	1606	Harbage (1603)
The Gentleman Usher	226	1606	Chambers, III, 251
The Queen's Arcadia	227	1606	Harbage (1605)
Nobody and Somebody	229	1606	Chambers, IV, 37
Caesar and Pompey (Caesar's Revenge)	232	1606	Chambers, III, 259
Wily Beguiled	234	1606	Chambers, IV, 53–54
Claudius Tiberius Nero (Tiberius)	240	1607	Chambers, IV, 5
The Fair Maid of the Exchange	242	1607	Chambers, IV,13
What You Will	252	1607	Chambers, III, 430
The Alexandraean Tragedy	260	1607	Chambers, III, 209
Julius Caesar (by Alexander)	261	1607	Chambers, III, 209
Mustapha	278	1609	Chambers, III, 331
The Case Is Altered	281	1609	Chambers, III, 357–358
Every Woman in Her Humour	283	1609	Chambers, IV, 11
Histriomastix	290	1610	Chambers, IV, 17–19
A Christian Turned Turk	300	1612	Chambers, III, 271
Mariam	308	1613	Chambers, III, 247
Cynthia's Revenge	314	1613	Chambers, III, 495
The Hog Hath Lost His Pearl	321	1614	Chambers, III, 496
Hymen's Triumph	325	1615	Chambers, III, 276–277
The Hector of Germany	329	1615	Chambers, III, 493
Albumazar	330	1615	Chambers, III, 498–499
The Four Prentices of London	333	1615	Chambers, III, 340–341
Englishmen for My Money (A Woman Will Have Her Will)	336	1616	Chambers, III, 334–335
The Two Gentlemen of Verona	391	1623	Chambers, *WS*, I, 329–331

The Comedy of Errors	393	1623	Chambers, *WS*, I, 305–312
All's Well That Ends Well	395	1623	Chambers, *WS*, I, 449–452
King John	398	1623	Chambers, *WS*, I, 364–367
1 Henry the Sixth	399	1623	Chambers, *WS*, I, 289–293
Coriolanus	401	1623	Chambers, *WS*, I, 478–480
Timon of Athens	402	1623	Chambers, *WS*, I, 480–484
Antony and Cleopatra	405	1623	Chambers, *WS*, I, 476–478
Nero (Piso's Conspiracy)	410	1624	Bentley, V, 1379–1382
Apollo Shroving	414	1627	Harbage (1627)
The Andrian Woman	415	1627	Bentley, IV, 946–947
The Eunuch	416	1627	Bentley, IV, 946–947
Aminta	417	1628	Bentley, V, 999
Lodovick Sforza	418	1628	Bentley, IV, 513–514
Albovine	422	1629	Bentley, III, 197–199
Aristippus	431	1630	Bentley, V, 971–973
2 The Honest Whore	435	1630	Chambers, III, 294–295
Hoffman	438	1631	Chambers, III, 264
The Spanish Bawd	439	1631	Bentley, IV, 727–728
Sicelides	443	1631	Chambers, III, 315
Caesar and Pompey	444	1631	Chambers, III, 259
1 The Fair Maid of the West	445	1631	Bentley, IV, 568
The Raging Turk	447	1631	Bentley, IV, 509–510
Rhodon and Iris	449	1631	Harbage (1631)
Antigone	450	1631	Bentley, IV, 833–834
The Courageous Turk	458	1632	Bentley, IV, 505–507
A New Wonder, a Woman Never Vexed	460	1632	Chambers, III, 474
The Rival Friends	465	1632	Bentley, IV, 534–536
The Jealous Lovers	469	1632	Bentley, V, 982–986
The Jew of Malta	475	1633	Chambers, III, 424–425; Bentley, IV, 573–574
A Match at Midnight	476	1633	Chambers, III, 474
Fuimus Troes	482	1633	Harbage (1625)
Orestes	485	1633	Bentley, IV, 507–509
Alaham	489	1633	Chambers, III, 331
The Noble Soldier	490	1634	Bentley, III, 257–260
Adrasta	501	1635	Bentley, IV, 603
The Wonder of a Kingdom	508	1636	Bentley, III, 273–275
The Vow Breaker	510	1636	Bentley, V, 1043–1045

The Royal King and the Loyal Subject	516	1637	Chambers, III, 341
The Valiant Scot	520	1637	Bentley, V, 1233–1236
A Shoemaker a Gentleman	531	1638	Chambers, III, 473–474
The Wise Woman of Hogsdon	535	1638	Chambers, III, 342
Love's Riddle	539	1638	Bentley, III, 179–180
Cleopatra	553	1639	Bentley, IV, 834–835
Julia Agrippina	554	1639	Bentley, IV, 837–838
The Sophister	556	1639	Bentley, V, 1277–1280
Imperiale	560	1639	Bentley, III, 469–470
The Phoenix in Her Flames	569	1639	Bentley, IV, 727
Christ's Passion	579	1640	Bentley, V, 1048
The Knave in Grain	580	1640	Bentley, III, 187–190
The Unfortunate Mother	581	1640	Bentley, IV, 942–944
The Strange Discovery	584	1640	Bentley, IV, 515–516
The Swaggering Damsel	589	1640	Bentley, III, 153–154
The Constant Maid (Love Will Find Out the Way)	592	1640	Bentley, V, 1095–96
1 Saint Patrick for Ireland	593	1640	Bentley, V, 1143–44
2 The Cid	596	1640	Bentley, V, 1031–1032
Sicily and Naples	599	1640	Bentley, IV, 531–532
Love Crowns the End	600	1640	Bentley, V, 1221–1222
The Antiquary	601	1641	Bentley, IV, 739–741
Landgartha	604	1641	Bentley, III, 97–98
Mercurius Brittanicus	605	1641	Harbage (1641)
Mortimer His Fall	615	1641	Bentley, IV, 621–622
The Sad Shepherd	618	1641	Bentley, IV, 625–628
Cola's Fury	626	1646	Harbage (1645)
Il Pastor Fido	629	1647	Harbage (1647)
The Country Girl	632	1647	Bentley, III, 5–8
Gripus and Hegio	633	1647	Harbage (1647)
The Nice Valour	652	1647	Bentley, III, 381–384
Women Pleased	664	1647	Bentley, III, 431–433
Wit at Several Weapons	666	1647	Chambers, III, 232
Valentinian	667	1647	Chambers, III, 229
Four Plays in One	670	1647	Chambers, III, 231
The Amorous War	671	1648	Bentley, IV, 845–847
Medea	675	1648	Harbage (1648)
Charles the First	680	1649	Harbage (1649)
Electra	683	1649	Harbage (1649)
Love in Its Ecstasy	685	1649	Bentley, IV, 952
The Rebellion of Naples	689	1649	Harbage (1649)
The Virgin Widow	690	1649	Bentley, IV, 957–959
The Guardian (Cutter of Coleman Street)	693	1650	Harbage (1642)
The Distracted State	694	1651	Bentley, V, 1219–1220

Astraea	695	1651	Harbage (1651)
Hippolytus	696	1651	Harbage (1651)
Marcus Tullius Cicero	698	1651	Harbage (1651)
Plutothalamia Plutogamia	699	1651	Harbage (1627)
The Lady Errant	701	1651	Bentley, III, 128–132
The Ordinary	702	1651	Bentley, III, 132–134
The Seige	703	1651	Bentley, III, 141–142
The Just General	704	1652	Harbage (1652)
The Bastard	707	1652	Bentley, IV, 500–501
The Loyal Lovers	709	1652	Harbage (1652)
Sophompaneas	710	1652	Harbage (1652)
The Scots Figgaries	711	1652	Harbage (1652)
The Fatal Contract (The Eunuch)	714	1653	Bentley, IV, 543–546
The Ghost	715	1653	Bentley, V, 1342
The Queen	716	1653	Bentley, III, 457–458
The City Wit	721	1653	Bentley, III, 59–61
The Damoiselle	722	1653	Bentley, III, 65–67
The Court Secret	728	1653	Bentley, V, 1100–1102
Alphonsus of Germany	729	1654	Bentley, V, 1285–1288; Harbage (1594)
Revenge for Honour	730	1654	Bentley, IV, 489–493
Ariadne	734	1654	Harbage (1654)
The Combat of Love and Friendship	735	1654	Bentley, IV, 851–852
The Extravagant Shepherd	737	1654	Harbage (1654)
Love's Dominion (Love's Kingdom)	738	1654	Harbage (1654)
Fortune by Land and Sea	739	1655	Chambers, III, 343
The Lovesick King	740	1655	Bentley, III, 43–45
The Poor Man's Comfort	741	1655	Bentley, III, 191–192
The Twins	742	1655	Bentley, V, 1008–1009
The Clouds	743	1655	Harbage (1655)
Mirza	744	1655	Harbage (1655)
Filli di Sciro	745	1655	Bentley, V, 1171
The Floating Island	746	1655	Bentley, V, 1189–1195
The Politician	752	1655	Bentley, V, 1137–1139
Polyeuclis	753	1655	Harbage (1655)
Actaeon and Diana	754	1655	Harbage (1653)
Oenone	756	1655	Harbage (1653)
The Careless Shepherdess	761	1656	Bentley, IV, 501–505
The Hectors	762	1656	Harbage (1656)
1 The Siege of Rhodes	763	1656	Harbage (1656)
Horatius	765	1656	Harbage (1656)
The Obstinate Lady	771	1657	Bentley, III, 168–170
The Queen's Exchange (The Royal Exchange)	772	1657	Bentley, III, 86–87
The False Favourite Disgraced	774	1657	Harbage (1657)

Lust's Dominion	777	1657	Chambers, III, 427
No Wit Like a Woman's	778	1657	Bentley, V, 1134
The Fool Would Be a Favourite	779	1657	Bentley, III, 117–118
Osmond the Great Turk	780	1657	Bentley, III, 119–122
Women Beware Women	782	1657	Bentley, IV, 905–907
Orgula	783	1658	Harbage (1658)
The Enchanted Lovers	790	1658	Harbage (1658)
Love and War	791	1658	Harbage (1658)
Love's Victory	792	1658	Harbage (1658)
The Unhappy Fair Irene	793	1658	Harbage (1658)
The Wandering Lover	794	1658	Harbage (1658)
Trappolin Creduto Principe	796	1658	Bentley, III, 170–172
The Shepherd's Paradise	797	1659	Bentley, IV, 917–921
1 Sir Francis Drake	798	1659	Harbage (1658)
The Blind Beggar of Bednal Green	801	1659	Chambers, III, 285
Lady Alimony	802	1659	Harbage (1659)
The Noble Ingratitude	804	1659	Harbage (1659)
The World's Idol, Plutus	805	1659	Harbage (1659)
The Lovesick Court	807	1659	Bentley, III, 76–77
The New Academy	809	1659	Bentley, 81 III,
The Queen and Concubine	810	1659	Bentley, III, 85–86
The Sad One	811	1659	Bentley, V, 1213–1214

Appendix C.

Dramatic Texts First Printed
1600–1659 Which Are Not Plays

Greg lists 171 other dramatic texts first printed in the years 1600–1659, but these are not included as evidence for my study because they are not plays. These works, identified only by Greg reference number, are listed below according to the Harbage classification.

Masque

207, 237, 238, 269, 270, 271, 280, 291, 309, 310, 319, 320, 324, 343, 344, 345, 347, 348, 349, 350, 358, 365, 381, 385, 407, 411, 437, 452, 453, 454, 488, 496, 497, 502, 514, 524, 526, 527, 543, 544, 571, 585, 595, 606, 607, 608, 609, 610, 611, 627, 634, 713, 768, 803

Pageant

218, 282, 288, 295, 302, 311, 322, 332, 335, 338, 351, 355, 359, 366, 367, 383, 387, 409, 413, 419, 421, 448, 466, 483, 495, 500, 522, 546, 566, 764, 775, 786, 800

Classical Legend

294, 313, 317, 467, 468, 504

Entertainment

200, 201, 202, 208, 233, 289, 312, 318, 339, 340, 341, 369, 370, 371, 372, 373, 374, 375, 376, 377, 378, 426, 487, 503, 511, 512, 612, 613, 614, 625, 731, 732, 770, 787, 789

Dialogue
  326, 331, 354, 361, 528, 529, 530, 602, 603, 623, 630, 631, 635, 636,
  672, 673, 676, 677, 678, 679, 682, 686, 687, 688, 691, 697
Tilt
  346
Moral
  190, 193, 194, 239, 353, 434, 473
Comic Interlude
  700, 748, 799
Droll
  757, 769
Medley
  776
Monologue
  432
Speech
  342

A Yorkshire Tragedy (272) is not included as evidence because it is
not a full-length play. See Baldwin Maxwell, *Studies in the Shakespeare
Apocrypha* (New York: King's Crown Press, 1956), pp. 138–196.

Notes

1. Introduction

1. The opening of the Globe is generally regarded as a landmark in theatrical history. By taking late 1599 as a *terminus a quo,* I eliminate only two plays of Shakespeare for which there is specific external evidence of performance: *The Comedy of Errors,* performed at Gray's Inn on 28 December 1594; and *Titus Andronicus* performed by Sussex's men on 24 and 28 January 1594 and 6 February 1594, and by the Admiral's or Chamberlain's men, or both, on 7 and 14 June 1594. Chambers, *WS,* II, 317–320. Concerning the Globe's opening date, Chambers notes, "It was doubtless ready for the occupation of the Chamberlain's men by the beginning of the autumn season of 1599. One of the earliest plays there produced by them was Shakespeare's *Julius Caesar* which on 21 September Thomas Platter crossed the river to see" Chambers, II, 415. In a later study Chambers states that Platter "does not name the Globe, but the theatre was south of the river, and the Swan was probably not in regular use. The Rose no doubt was, but as the Admiral's had new Caesar plays in 1594–5 and again in 1602, they are not very likely to have been staging one in 1599. Platter's 'at least fifteen characters' agrees fairly with *Julius Caesar,* on the assumption that he disregarded a number of inconspicuous parts. The date of 1599 fits in well with other evidence." *WS,* I, 397. See also Ernest Schanzer, "Thomas Platter's Observations on the Elizabethan Stage," *N & Q,* n.s. 3:465–467(1956).

2. Listed below are the contemporary references to performances of Shakespeare's plays by his company in the years between late 1599 and 1642 as cited by Chambers, *WS,* II, 322–353; original spellings and variant titles have been retained: "Keyser Julio Caesare," London, 1599; "Sir John Old Castell," probably at Hunsdon House, Blackfriars, 6 March 1599/1600; "Kyng Harry the iiijth, and of the kyllyng of Kyng Richard the second," the Globe, 17 February 1600/1; "Twelve Night, or What You Will," Middle Temple, 2 February

141

1601/2; "As You Like It," Wilton, 1603; "The Moor of Venis," Whitehall, 1 November 1604; "The Merry Wives of Winsor," Whitehall, 4 November 1604; "Mesur for Mesur," Whitehall, 26 December 1604; "The Plaie of Errors," Whitehall, 28 December 1604; "Loves Labour Lost," Whitehall "Betwin Newers Day and Twelfe Day," 1604/5; "Henry the Fift," Whitehall, 7 January 1604/5; "The Marthant of Venis," Whitehall, 10 February 1604/5; "The Martchant of Venis," Whitehall, 12 February 1604/5; "Pericles," London, 1608?; "More de Venise," the Globe, 30 April 1610; "Mackbeth," the Globe, 20 April 1611; "Cimbalin King of England," London, 1611; "Richard the 2," the Globe, 30 April 1611; "The Winters Talle," the Globe, 15 May 1611; "The Tempest," Whitehall, 1 November 1611; "Ye Winters Nightes Tayle," Whitehall, 5 November 1611; "Much Adoe Abowte Nothinge," "The Tempest," "The Winters Tale," "Sir John Falstaffe," "The Moore of Venice," "Caesars Tragedye," "The Hotspur," and "Benedicte and Betteris," payment warrant for performances at Court dated 20 May 1613; "All Is True, representing some principal pieces of the reign of Henry VIII," the Globe, 29 June 1613; "Twelfte Night," Court, 6 April 1618; "The Winter's Tale," Court, 7 April 1618; "Pirrocles, Prince of Tyre," Whitehall, 20 May 1619; "The Winters Tale," "The 2 Noble Kinesmen," "The Tradgedy of Ham[let]," and "[Seco]nd Part of Falstaff," probably considered for performance at Court, ca. 1619–20; "Malvolio," Court, 2 February 1622/3; "Winter's Tale," Revels license, 19 August 1623; "The Winters Tale," Whitehall, 18 January 1623/4; "The First Part of Sir John Falstaff," Whitehall, 1 January 1624/5; "King Henry 8," the Globe, 29 July 1628; "The Moor of Venise," Blackfriars?, 22 November 1629; "Pericles," the Globe, 10 June 1631; "Richard Ye Seconde," the Globe, 12 June 1631; "Richarde the Thirde," St. James, 16 November 1633; "The Taminge of the Shrewe," Court, 26 November 1633; "Cymbeline," Court, 1 January 1633/4; "The Winters Tale," Court, 16 January 1633/4; "Ye More of Venice," Blackfriars, 6 May 1635; "The Moore of Venice," Hampton Court, 8 December 1636; "Hamlett," Hampton Court, 24 January 1636/7; "The Tragedie of Cesar," St. James, 31 January 1636/7; "Ould Castel," the Cockpit-in-Court, 29 May 1638; "Ceaser," the Cockpit-in-Court, 13 November 1638; "The Mery Wifes of Winsor," the Cockpit-in-Court, 15 November 1638.

Chambers notes that Shakespeare's company appeared at least once in each of the following places during the period 1599–1616: Oxford, Bath, Shrewsbury, Coventry, Ipswich, Leicester, Marlborough, Dover, Maidstone, Barnstaple, Dunwich, Hythe, New Romney, Stafford, Sudbury, Winchester, Nottingham. *WS*, II, 322–345. Bentley notes that the King's men appeared at least once in each of the following places during the period 1617–1642: Oxford, Ipswich, Winchester, Stratford-on-Avon, Marlborough, Reading, Leicester, Coventry, Nottingham, Dover, Saffron Walden, Worcester, Craven District, Canterbury, Bristol, Doncaster, Southampton, Dunwich, Windsor. Bentley, I, 92–93. The need for flexibility in staging procedures, especially on tour, is well documented by W. F. Rothwell, "Was There a Typical Elizabethan Stage?" *Shakespeare Survey*, 12:15–21(1959).

3. Gerald Eades Bentley, *Shakespeare and His Theatre* (Lincoln: University

of Nebraska Press, 1964), p. 85. Of the 276 plays included as evidence for the present study, 131 were first acted before 1621, while 145 were first acted in the years 1621–1642. Of the 87 plays that can be acted with minimal equipment, 29 were first acted before 1621, while 58 were first acted in the years 1621–1642. Of the 45 plays that need only an acting place above the stage in addition to entrances and large properties, 19 were first acted before 1621, while 26 were first acted in the years 1621–1642. Of the 102 plays that need an accessory space covered with a movable door or hangings, 56 plays were first acted before 1621, while 46 were first acted in the years 1621–1642. Of the 42 plays that require access to a place below, 28 were first acted before 1621, while 14 were first acted in the years 1621–1642. These figures indicate that except for an increase in the proportion of plays that can be acted with minimal equipment, there were few differences between the staging procedures for plays first acted before 1621 and for those first acted in the years 1621–1642.

4. These drawings are reproduced by Chambers, IV, 359–362. Although masques at Court and plays acted by amateurs provided occasional scenic innovations, there appears to be no development in the staging procedures for plays written for public performance by English professional actors before 1642. The King's men probably acted with scenery—but at Court rather than at the Globe or Blackfriars—in the following plays: *Pallantus and Endora* (537), "Design'd for an entertainment of the King and Queen at *York*-House" in 1634/5 (Bentley, IV, 691–694); *The Royal Slave* (570), Oxford and Court, 1636 (Bentley, III, 134–141); *Aglaura* (541), Court 1637/8 (Bentley, V, 1201–1207); *The Queen of Aragon* (588), Court, 1640 (Bentley, IV, 522–525). Queen Henrietta's men first acted Heywood's *Love's Mistress or The Queen's Masque* (504), at the Phoenix in November 1634 (Bentley, IV, 582). They later acted the same work at Court with sets and effects by Inigo Jones, but there is no evidence that these settings were used at the Phoenix. See T. J. King, "The Staging of Plays at the Phoenix in Drury Lane, 1617–1642," *TN*, 19:146–166(1965). My findings run counter to Lily B. Campbell's statement: "that the spectacular representation of the drama was coming to be considered as possible in the public theatres as well as at court is indicated in many ways . . . But it must be noted that in every case in which we are certain that plays were presented with movable scenes [before 1640] they were shown at Blackfriars, the Phoenix (or Cockpit), or Salisbury Court." Campbell, *Scenes and Machines on the English Stage during the Renaissance* (Cambridge: Cambridge University Press, 1923), p. 206. The early development of scenery for masques at Court is amply discussed and illustrated by Richard Southern, *Changeable Scenery: Its Origin and Development in the British Theatre* (London: Faber and Faber, 1952). See also Kenneth R. Richards, "Changeable Scenery for Plays on the Caroline Stage," *TN*, 23:6–20(Autumn 1968).

5. Charles T. Prouty, "An Early Elizabethan Playhouse," *Shakespeare Survey*, 6:64–74(1953), p. 71.

6. Greg, *Documents*, I, x–xi.

7. J. W. Saunders describes one of his textual problems in attempting to isolate Globe plays for special study: "There are relatively few plays which

we can certainly identify as Globe plays, and even these exist only in 'corrupt' texts. I make use of terms like 'corruption' in a different sense from the bibliographers: a 'bad quarto,' in their sense, may be a good text for the historian of the stage, if it reflects accurately the staging practices of only one theatre." Saunders, "Staging at the Globe, 1599–1613," *SQ*, 11:401(1960). But in selecting the plays for textual evidence, Saunders does not take into account significant bibliographical studies by Greg, Bald, and others; nor does he give complete information about performances of these plays at places other than the Globe before printing.

8. R. B. McKerrow, "The Elizabethan Printer and Dramatic Manuscripts," *Library*, 4th ser. 12:270–272(1931). See also R. B. McKerrow, "A Suggestion Regarding Shakespeare's Manuscripts," *RES*, 2:459–465(1935).

9. One should, however, keep in mind Greg's caveat about determining the probable source of printer's copy for playbooks: "We enter . . . a misty mid region of Weir, a land of shadowy shapes and melting outlines, where not even the most patient inquiry and the most penetrating analysis can hope to arrive at any but tentative and proximate conclusions." Greg, *Folio*, p. 105. Fredson Bowers suggests thirteen possible classes of printer's copy, of which numbers (5) and (6) are of most value for the study of stage conditions: "The copy, on the evidence, seems to have been of every conceivable variety, but it falls into the following major classes, some of them speculative: (1) author's foul papers; (2) authorial or scribal fair copies not intended for direct theatrical use; (3) foul papers or fair copies partially marked by the prompter as a preliminary for transcription into prompt; (4) scribal transcripts made for private individuals and not for theatrical purposes, the source being foul papers, fair copy, or theatrical prompt book; (5) a manuscript prompt book itself; (6) a scribal transcript of a prompt book; (7) an unrevised copy of an earlier printed edition; (8) an unauthoritatively revised copy of an earlier printed edition, the revisions presumably originating with the publisher or his agent; (9) an authoritatively revised copy of an earlier edition marked by the author; (10) a copy of an earlier printed edition annotated by comparison with some manuscript, usually assumed to be authorial or prompt, preserved in the theatre's archives; (11) a subdivision of the above, consisting of an earlier printed edition marked and used by the theatre company as a prompt book, or another copy of an edition marked for the printer to conform to such a printed prompt book; (12) another possible subdivision of the above, a new and as yet untested theory, which conjectures a scribal transcript made for the printer of such a marked printed prompt book, or else a manuscript made up for the printer by an independent act of conflating a printed edition with a manuscript preserved in the theatre; (13) the 'foul papers,' fair copy, prompt book, or transcript of a prompt book of a memorial reconstruction of the text without direct transcriptional link with any manuscript derived from author's autograph, in other words, the copy for a so-called 'bad quarto.'" Bowers, *On Editing Shakespeare*, (Charlottesville: University Press of Virginia, 1966), pp. 11–12.

Wilfred T. Jewkes offers conjectures concerning the "textual origin" of "all [extant] plays acted between 1583 and 1616." His summary lists three plays that he considers to be "probably printed from a company's prompt-book": *The Atheist's Tragedy, The Coxcomb,* and *The Two Noble Kinsmen.* His category of plays "probably printed from copy which had in some way been annotated for performance" is too ambiguous to be useful for my study. Jewkes, *Act Division in Elizabethan and Jacobean Plays, 1583–1616* (Hamden, Conn.: Shoe String Press, 1958), pp. 337–352.

10. Adams, *Herbert,* pp. 20–21, 53. In discussing the censorship of this play, Bald states that apparently the words "piss" and "pispots" were among the "foule and offensive matters" to which Herbert lodged objections. The Folio substitutes "unready" (I.i) and "looking-glasses" (IV.i). Bald, *Folio,* pp. 68–69.

11. Bald, *Folio,* p. 60. Earlier Bald described this manuscript as follows: "*The Womans Prize* occupies 101 pages, and is written throughout in an impeccable italic hand which at first sight seems to belong to the eighteenth rather than to the seventeenth century. The complete absence of the long *s* is particularly noticeable. There are, however, a few corrections in an undoubted seventeenth-century hand, and reference to the copy-books of the writing-masters of the first half of the century shows that such hands, though rarely met with, were actually taught. One may conjecture that the transcriber of the play was probably himself a writing-master. The spelling of the manuscript makes it fairly certain that it belongs to a date probably earlier than 1650, and it must be borne in mind that although there was a very real demand for such transcripts before 1647 they had no *raison d'être* after the appearance of the folio." Bald, *Folio,* pp. 51–52.

12. Bald, *Folio,* pp. 77–78. I interpret "draw all the curtains close" in the Folio as an order to close the curtains on Livia's bedstead, for which a chair was substituted in MS. See Richard Hosley, "The Staging of Desdemona's Bed," *SQ,* 14:57–65(1963).

13. Greg, *Folio,* p. 411.

14. Chambers, III, 366–368.

15. Although music and off-stage sounds are important effects in almost every play considered here, I have not discussed such matters because music and sound are not dependent on the structure of the stage or playhouse. For useful studies of theatrical music, see John H. Long, *Shakespeare's Use of Music: A Study of the Music and its Performance in the Original Production of Seven Comedies* (Gainesville: University of Florida Press, 1955), and his *Shakespeare's Use of Music: The Final Comedies* (Gainesville: University of Florida Press, 1961). Sounds are discussed by Frances A. Shirley, *Shakespeare's Use of Off-Stage Sounds* (Lincoln: University of Nebraska Press, 1963).

2. Entrances and Large Properties

1. Five other texts require more than two entrances, but none of these texts depends on prompt copy: *Eastward Ho* (217), (Chapman et al., 1605; Chambers, III, 254–256), *Enter Maister Touch-stone, and Quick-silver at Severall*

dores, Quick-silver with his hat, pumps, short sword and dagger, and a Racket trussed up under his cloake. At the middle dore, Enter Golding discovering a Gold-smiths shoppe, and walking short turns before it (I.i.); *The Travels of the Three English Brothers* (248), (Day, 1607; Chambers, III, 286–287), *Enter three severall waies the three Brothers* (H4v); *The Roaring Girl* (298), (Dekker, 1611; Chambers, III, 296–297), *The three shops open in a ranke* (C3); *Covent Garden* (542), (Nabbes, 1638; Bentley, IV, 932–934), *Enter Dungworth, Ralph, and Dobson, as newly come to Towne by the right Scoene* (I.i), *Enter Littleword and Mris. Tongall, by the middle Scoene* (I.v), *Enter Ralph and Dobson by the left Scoene* (III.iii); *Bartholmew Fair* (455), (Jonson, collection 1631; Chambers, III, 372–373), which refers specifically to five places on the stage and is discussed by Eugene M. Waith, "The Staging of *Bartholomew Fair*," *Studies in English Literature, 1500–1900,* 2:181–195(1962).

An unlocalized stage façade with three entrances is seen in the Jones/Webb drawings for an unidentified pre-Restoration playhouse (Plate IX) and in the illustrations for Robert Fludd's Latin treatise *Ars Memoriae,* printed in Germany in 1619, which were first linked to the English theater by Robert Bernheimer, "Another Globe Theatre," *SQ,* 9:19–29(1958). The pictures are also discussed by Frances Yates, "New Light on the Globe Theatre," *New York Review of Books,* May 26, 1966, pp. 16–21; I. A. Shapiro, "Robert Fludd's Stage-Illustration," *Shakespeare Studies,* 2:192–209(1967). Three entrances in the stage façade are suggested by Richard Hosley, "A Reconstruction of the Second Blackfriars," in *The Elizabethan Theatre,* ed. David Galloway (Toronto: Macmillan of Canada, 1969), pp. 74–88. If hangings are added for scenes in which they are required and if the stage has a trap to the place below, the equipment shown in those three drawings can serve the needs of all 276 texts included as evidence for this study.

Although the Swan drawing shows only two stage doors in the tiring-house façade, George F. Reynolds, *The Staging of Elizabethan Plays at the Red Bull Theater, 1605–1625,* (New York: Modern Language Association, 1940) states: "Red Bull plays, in spite of their use of spectacle, could be given on a stage structurally like that of the Swan, with the single important addition of a third stage door" (p. 188). In supporting this statement, however, Reynolds admits: "Proof that the Red Bull had at least three doors leading from the tiring-house to the stage is not as plentiful as one might expect" (p. 109). He cites the text of only one play that specifically requires three doors: *The Four Prentices of London* (333), (Heywood, printed 1615; Chambers, III, 340–341, gives 1592? as probable date of composition), *Enter three in blacke clokes at three doores* (Prologue). Reynolds also cites the moral masque *The World Tossed at Tennis* (365), (Middleton and William Rowley, printed 1620; Bentley, IV, 907–911), *Enter at the three severall doores the nine Worthies, three after three.* This masque cannot be considered typical of plays performed at the Red Bull, however; the Induction states that the work was "prepar'd for his Majesties Entertainment at Denmarke-House."

Bernard Beckerman, *Shakespeare at the Globe, 1599–1609* (New York: Macmillan, 1962), also notes that evidence for a third access is very thin: "For the existence of a third entry the Globe plays offer no conclusive proof. No stage direction specifying an entry from a middle door, such as can be found in non-Globe plays, appears. However, certain scenes do suggest the use of a third entrance. In *Macbeth* (V.vii), Malcolm, who has presumably come through one door (A), is invited into the castle of Dunsinane by Siward. At his exit (through B presumably) Macbeth enters. Either he can come from the door (A) through which Malcolm entered, which is dramatically unconvincing, or from the door (B) of Dunsinane, which is awkward, or from a third entrance, evidence for which is not conclusive" (p. 70). However, Macbeth's entrance through door (A) after the exit of Malcolm through (B) would be "dramatically unconvincing" only if one does not accept the Elizabethan convention that when the stage is cleared of actors and properties, any designation of place suggested by the preceding scene is nullified. Thus, the fictional setting of Folio V.vii moves from an unlocalized battle scene between Macbeth and Young Siward, to an unlocalized Macduff soliloquy, to Malcolm and Siward before the "castle," to another unlocalized battle as Macbeth re-enters and is soon confronted by Macduff. In watching pursuits and killings, and in hearing loud *alarums,* the audience is much more concerned with the action than with its exact fictional locale.

2. Another interpretation is suggested by Allardyce Nicoll, who states that "the most reasonable, effective and practical interpretation of the phrase 'pass over the stage' is a move from yard to platform to yard again." Nicoll, "Passing Over the Stage," *Shakespeare Survey,* 12:53(1959). However, this direction is found in many plays performed at Court where there was no yard, and at other places where perhaps there was no platform stage.

3. See R. A. Foakes and R. T. Rickert, eds., *Henslowe's Diary* (Cambridge: Cambridge University Press, 1961), *passim;* Albert Feuillerat, "Documents Relating to the Office of the Revels in the Time of Queen Elizabeth," in W. Bang, ed., *Materialen zur kunde des alteren Englischen Dramas,* XXI (Louvain, 1908), *passim;* Albert Feuillerat, "Documents Relating to the Revels at Court in the Time of King Edward VI and Queen Mary" (The Losely MSS.), in W. Bang, ed., *Materialen zur kunde des alteren Englischen Dramas,* XLIV (Louvain, 1914), *passim.*

3. Above the Stage

1. The evidence offered in this chapter supports the findings of Richard Hosley, who has published three excellent articles on the use of this acting area: "The Upper Stage in *Romeo and Juliet,*" *SQ,* 5:371–379(1954); "The Gallery over the Stage in the Public Playhouse of Shakespeare's Time," *SQ,* 8:15–31(1957); "Shakespeare's Use of a Gallery over the Stage," *Shakespeare Survey,* 10:77–89(1957). See also, Herbert Berry, "The Playhouse in the Boar's Head Inn, Whitechapel," in *The Elizabethan Theatre,* ed. David Galloway (Toronto: Macmillan of Canada, 1969), pp. 45–73.

2. A sketch by Inigo Jones for the masque *Tempe Restored* (1632) shows Jove on an eagle with thunderbolts in his hand, but the drawing does not indicate whether flying machinery was used to make a descent. The sketch is reproduced by Allardyce Nicoll, *Stuart Masques and the Renaissance Stage* (New York: Benjamin Blom, 1938), p. 94. C. Walter Hodges, *The Globe Restored,* rev. ed. (New York: Coward-McCann, 1968) reproduces a drawing for flying machinery that "may have been copied from the work of the famous Giacomo Torelli at a theater in Venice between 1640 and 1645" (p. 138). Concerning the use of such equipment on the English stage, John Cranford Adams, *The Globe Playhouse,* 2nd ed. (New York: Barnes and Noble, 1961), pp. 365, 335, cites Ben Jonson's Prologue for *Every Man in His Humour* (Folio, 1616): "Where neither *Chorus* wafts you ore the seas/Nor creaking throne comes downe the boys to please," and stage directions in Greene's *Alphonsus of Aragon,* which Chambers (III, 327) dates ca. 1587 without conjecture about company or playhouse: *After you have sounded thrise, let Venus be let downe, from the top of the Stage, and when she is downe, say . . . Exit Venus. Or if you can conveniently, let a chaire come downe, from the top of the stage, and draw her up.* Adams (p. 336) also cites the following stage directions: *The Variety* (Cavendish, ca. 1639, Bentley, III, 149–151) has *Musick Throne descends* (IV); *The Ball* (Shirley, 1632, Bentley, V, 1076–1079) has *A golden Ball descends, Enter Venus and Cupid* (V); *A Wife for a Month* (Fletcher, 1624, Bentley, III, 422–425) has *Cupid and the Graces ascend in the Chariot* (II). In addition, Adams cites some ambiguous dialogue allusions in *The Seven Champions of Christendom* (Kirke, 1635, Bentley, IV, 712–714) and an episode in *Englishmen for My Money* (Haughton, 1598, Chambers, III, 334–335) in which Vandalle is raised in a basket halfway up to a window and left stranded; the next morning he is lowered to the ground (pp. 342–343). Richard Hosley, "The Staging of the Monument Scenes in *Antony and Cleopatra,*" *The University of Pennsylvania Library Chronicle,* 30:62–71(1964), cites this action in *Englishmen for My Money* as precedent for hoisting Antony in a basket when *They heave Anthony aloft to Cleopatra* (IV.xv.37). Neither play mentions machinery, and there is no evidence as to where and when *Antony and Cleopatra* may have been performed. Chambers, *WS,* I, 476–478. Greg states that this text was "printed from Shakespeare's foul papers." Greg, *Folio,* p. 402. Thus, while there is no proof for Beckerman's comment that "no machinery for flying either actors or properties existed" (*Shakespeare at the Globe* p. 106), it can be stated with some certainty that such machinery was not *required* in the vast majority of plays, which suggests that it was also not available in the vast majority of playhouses.

3. Foakes and Rickert, eds., *Henslowe's Diary,* pp. 319, 86.

4. DeWitt T. Starnes and Ernest William Talbert, *Classical Myth and Legend in Renaissance Dictionaries* (Chapel Hill: University of North Carolina Press, 1955), cite a seventeenth century dictionary of mythology as follows: "Howsoever it be, the fable doth present unto us the picture of an inconsiderate and ambitious Prince, who being touched with an eager desire of Majesty, before

his time ascends the Throne, but shortly after, letting loose the reins by his undiscreet Government, he sets his subjects all in a combustion, and indangers his own downfall" (p. 120). In Shakespeare's *Richard II* (first printed 1597) the King *on the walls* is summoned to "the base court" to meet with Bolingbroke. Richard's speech beginning "Down, down I come, like glist'ring Phaeton" (III.iii.186) may be given as he descends on a stairway in view of the audience. In all the early texts of the play Richard remains on stage until *exeunt* at the end of the scene. Capell (1768) and later editors emend with *Exeunt from above* (l. 191) and *Enter King Richard and his Attendants below* (l. 195).

4. Doors or Hangings

1. C. Walter Hodges, *passim*, and George F. Reynolds, pp. 131–132.

2. For a useful discussion of this accessory area, see Richard Hosley, "The Discovery Space in Shakespeare's Globe," *Shakespeare Survey*, 12:35–46(1959).

5. Below the Stage

1. Prouty, "An Early Elizabethan Playhouse," p. 71.

2. In *Macbeth* the Murderer says that Banquo is "safe in a ditch" (III.iv.26), which suggests that his body was thrown in the trap. After the murder there is no indication that the Murderers bear the body offstage (III.ii.22).

3. Henslowe notes that he "Bowght a robe for to goo invisibell" for the Admiral's men sometime after 3 April 1598. *Henslowe's Diary*, p. 325. I interpret the phrase *on the top* as the equivalent of *atop* and *above*.

4. The *quient device* need not be complex. A *cloath* is used on the banquet table in *The Spanish Curate* (V.i), and presumably this would also be used for *The Tempest*. One means of making the banquet *vanish* would be to fasten the property food and drink to a second, false table cloth spread over the first cloth and firmly attached to the upstage edge of the table top. If Ariel stands between the table and the audience as he *claps his wings,* the false cloth can then be quickly flipped back so that when Ariel steps aside the audience sees only the bare first cloth on the table.

6. Twelfth Night at the Middle Temple

1. Cited by J. Bruce Williamson, *The History of the Temple, London* (London: J. Murray, 1924), p. 239.

2. Chambers, *WS*, II, 346.

3. Greg, *Folio*, pp. 296–297.

4. Richard Hosley suggests that for performances at the Middle Temple a platform stage mounted on four-foot trestles was placed in front of—and presumably behind—the hall screen. Hosley, "The Origins of the Shakespearian Playhouse," in *Shakespeare 400,* ed. James G. McManaway (New York: Holt, Rinehart and Winston, 1964), p. 33. If, however, *Twelfth Night* were acted

at mealtime, as John Manningham's *Diary* implies, a stage would not be needed because most of the audience would be seated at table and have adequate sight lines to the play acted at floor level. Another possibility is that the play was acted at the West or upper end of the hall, where the actors rigged a traverse or hangings to provide a space *within*. In either case, two entrances and a place-less façade can serve the staging needs of this play. F. E. Halliday, *A Shakespeare Companion 1564–1964,* rev. ed. (New York: Schocken Books, 1964), Plate 31 (b), shows Donald Wolfit's production of *Twelfth Night* at the Middle Temple Hall 2 February 1951. According to the photograph, the play was acted on a platform at the West end of the hall.

J. Bruce Williamson, *Middle Temple Hall* (London: Chancery Lane Press, 1928) prints a ground plan of the hall and gives the following dimensions: "Including the passage under the Gallery at the East or lower end, the Hall measures in length 101 feet 3 inches, in height from the floor to the level of the wall plate 30 feet and to the apex of the roof 57 feet 6 inches, and in width 40 feet 9 inches except where at the two bays 15 feet 7 inches more are added on the South and 10 feet 7 inches on the North side. The sumptuous screen with its rich carvings which supports the gallery was erected in 1574 and its elegant double-leaved doors were added in 1671" (p. 8). *Twelfth Night* does not require a trap to a place below. G. P. V. Akrigg, "*Twelfth Night* at the Middle Temple," *SQ,* 9:422–424(1958), points out the reference to "bay windows" (IV.ii.40) for further evidence that the play was first performed at the Middle Temple.

As part of the quatercentenary celebration of the opening of Middle Temple Hall, the Inn invited the Oxford and Cambridge Shakespeare Company to per-form *Twelfth Night* there for three nights, 4–6 March 1970. *The Law Guardian* (London), May 1970, reports: "H. M. Queen Elizabeth the Queen Mother, a Master of the Bench, who as Treasurer in 1949 had reopened the Hall after its repair from war damage, came to the first night." The play was reportedly acted in front of the hall screen, with the audience seated on scaffolding at the upper end of the hall.

Index of Plays

151

Index of Persons

Abrams, William Amos, 62
Adams, John Cranford, 122–123, 124, 148
Adams, Joseph Quincy, x; *Herbert,* 16, 32, 47, 63, 90; *Shakespearean Playhouses,* 119
Akrigg, G. P. V., 150
Alabaster, William, x
Albright, Victor E., 119
Archdale, Mervyn, 49
Armin, Robert, 22

Bald, Robert Cecil, 22, 49, 81, 144; *Folio,* 6–8, 13, 16, 27, 34–35, 41–42, 47, 50, 51, 70, 84, 92, 127, 145; *Hengist,* 47
Bang, W., 147
Barish, Jonas A., 21
Barnes, Barnabe, 89
Barry, Lording, 64
Bawcutt, N. W., 35
Beaumont, Francis, 5–6, 7, 15, 22, 32, 34, 42, 61, 65, 90
Beckerman, Bernard, 129–131, 146–147, 148
Bentley, Gerald Eades, 9, 17; *Jacobean and Caroline Stage,* Vol. I, 15, 22, 26, 34, 62, 84, 90, 142; Vol. III, 13, 16, 17, 22, 23, 24, 25, 26, 27, 28, 33, 34, 35, 40, 41, 42, 48, 50, 51, 65, 66, 67, 68, 70, 71, 81, 90, 91, 92, 93, 123, 127, 135, 136, 137, 138, 143, 148; Vol. IV, 13, 14, 15,
16, 23, 24, 25, 26, 27, 28, 31, 35, 40, 41, 42, 47, 48, 51, 67, 68, 69, 71, 80, 91, 123, 135, 136, 137, 138, 143, 145, 148; Vol. V, x, 14, 23–24, 25, 26, 27, 28, 65, 67, 68, 69, 70, 71, 80, 91, 92, 123, 135, 136, 137, 138, 143, 148; Vol. VI, xi; *Shakespeare and His Theatre,* 2, 142–143
Berkeley, William, 47, 81
Bernheimer, Robert, 146
Berry, Herbert, 147
Bertram, Paul, 83
Bowers, Fredson: *B&F,* 34, 65; *Dekker,* 14, 17, 21–22, 39–40, 48, 60–61, 62, 67, 82–83, 89, 90; *On Editing Shakespeare,* 144
Bradbrook, Muriel C., 119
Brome, Alexander, 42
Brome, Richard, 28, 33–34, 41, 42, 67, 70, 71
Brooke, Nicholas, 82
Brown, A., 14
Brown, J. R., 64, 90–91
Buck, Sir George, 46–47, 65

Campbell, Lily B., 143
Carlell, Lodowick, 22–23, 28, 67, 91–92
Cauthen, Irby B., Jr., 34
Cavendish, William, 27, 148
Chambers, Edmund K., 9; *The Elizabethan Stage,* Vol. II, x, 141; Vol. III, 14, 15, 19, 20, 21, 22, 26, 32, 34, 39, 40, 47, 48, 49, 60, 61, 62,

158

Index of Subjects

161